'With this welcome new addition to the growing body of solution focused literature, Judith Milner and Steve Myers offer a very practical guide to solution focused practice with a range of client groups – whether this is with young children or elderly people living with dementia, and everyone in-between. The ideas are clearly articulated and illustrated with dialogue. Traditional methods from the founders of solution focused brief therapy are integrated with modern developments. Practical exercises reinforce the learning and help to locate the skills within the reader's own practice. I can recommend this book to those who are new to this elegant and effective way of helping people as well as "old hands" such as myself who always can benefit from being brought back to basics.'
– *Andrew Callcott MA (SFBT), psychological therapist and former Chair of the UK Association for Solution Focused Practice*

'*Creative Ideas for Solution Focused Practice* provides busy practitioners with an integrated, flexible model which links theory, context and skills that are underpinned by sound values and principles. The book is refreshingly grounded in the authors' practice experience and promotes an approach to working with people that encourages change and growth that is strength based, collaborative and outcome focused. The exercises are easily adaptable to a range of practice scenarios and the book is a great reminder that "once we know what works, do more of it!" This is an excellent, easy-to-read resource written in an engaging style, which will inform and inspire all of us who are seeking to help and support people make better choices and lead rewarding lives.'
– *Dave Basker, Head of Quality and Practice Improvement, Children's Services, Leeds City Council*

'I would recommend this book to anyone developing skills for solution focused work in any aspect of client work.'
– *Dr Alasdair J. Macdonald, retired consultant psychiatrist and family therapist; chair of a Dorset counselling charity*

Creative Ideas for Solution Focused Practice

Creative Ideas for Solution Focused Practice

Inspiring Guidance,
Ideas and Activities

Judith Milner and
Steve Myers

Jessica Kingsley *Publishers*
London and Philadelphia

First published in 2017
by Jessica Kingsley Publishers
73 Collier Street
London N1 9BE, UK
and
400 Market Street, Suite 400
Philadelphia, PA 19106, USA

www.jkp.com

Library of Congress Cataloging in Publication Data
Title: Creative ideas for solution focused practice : inspiring guidance,
  ideas, and activities / Judith Milner and Steve Myers.
Description: London ; Philadelphia : Jessica Kingsley Publishers, 2017. |
  Includes bibliographical references and index.
Identifiers: LCCN 2016041505 (print) | LCCN 2016043011 (ebook) | ISBN
  9781785922176 (alk. paper) | ISBN 9781784504977 (ebook)
Subjects: | MESH: Counseling--methods | Interview, Psychological--methods
Classification: LCC RC488 (print) | LCC RC488 (ebook) | NLM WM 55 | DDC
  616.89/15--dc23
LC record available at https://lccn.loc.gov/2016041505

British Library Cataloguing in Publication Data
A CIP catalogue record for this book is available from the British Library

ISBN 978 1 78592 217 6
eISBN 978 1 78450 4977

Printed and bound in Great Britain

Contents

Introduction   *11*

1   Solution Focused Philosophy   13

Practice principles and assumptions   22
Practice principles   33
Empathy   33
Validating emotions with a hint of possibilities
(Rogers with a twist)   37
Listening   38

2   Practice Principles and Techniques   58

Beginning the conversation   59
Externalising the problem   68
Exceptions   71
Strengths   79
Developing goals   90
Evaluating the session   128

3   Specific Contexts   133

Terminally ill people   133
Suicide   137
People with chronic illness or disability   141
People who hear voices   143
People who are disabled with stress   146

4 Surviving Trauma and Violence   **148**

Survival questions   150
Survival of poor parenting scale   151
Safety and control   153
Bedtime therapy   154
6, 5, 4, 3, 2, 1   157
Being sensibly selfish   158
Doormat therapy   160
Comfort cues   161
Treats   164
Living well is the best revenge   164

Internet Resources   *167*
References   *168*
Index   *171*

List of Exercises

Good things 15

Sparkling moments. 16

Introductions and best hopes 17

Identifying skills 19

Off the wall questions. 21

Problems to solutions 27

Ever appreciating circles 28

From pathologies to descriptions .30

Solution focused scavenger hunt .32

From emotion to behaviour 1. 35

From emotion to behaviour 2. 36

Curious questioning 40

communicating clearly 41

Word watching 1 42

Word watching 2 43

Reframing the problem/diagnosis .44

Transparency 1 47

Transparency 2 48

Transparency with children in child protection work 52

The three houses 53

Transparency with adults in child protection work 54

Challenging problem talk. 61

Keeping solution focused. 63
Individualising the problem. 69
Exception finding 73
Devising a task 78
Focusing on strengths. 80
Success and failure 81
Searching for strengths. 84
Eliciting skills 85
Eliciting strengths 1 88
Eliciting strengths 2 89
Developing clear goals. 92
Goal setting with people who are violent to their partners . .94
The miracle question. 99
Goal setting 113
A scaling walk 120
More scaling. 121
Yet more scaling 122
Scaling a project. 123
Assessing confidence 127
Personalising scaled questions 128
Dilemmas. 136
Hope from despair 140
Solutions for you. 156
Curious questioning 159
Comfort cues 163

Introduction

This book is for the busy practitioner who needs reminding of their skills, creativity and successes in working in solution focused ways. It is primarily written for those who have some experience and understanding of the model. If you are new to solution focused practice we recommend our earlier texts which introduce the beginner to the principles, techniques and practices (Milner 2001; Myers 2007). The accessible exercises and examples we present in this book are drawn from practice experience and will provide ideas and inspiration for the further development of your own expertise in working with people in solution focused ways.

1

Solution Focused Philosophy

'If it ain't broke, don't fix it.
Once you know what works, do more of it.
If it doesn't work, don't do it again.
Do something different.'

(BERG AND MILLER 1992, P.17)

This pithy statement neatly encapsulates the ways in which solution focused practice views and engages with the problems that people experience. Developed primarily by Steve de Shazer and others at the Brief Therapy Family Center in Milwaukee, US (1988, 1991), solution focused practice has been used in a range of situations where people present with problems such as poor behaviour, mental ill health, relationship difficulties, violence, substance misuse and a variety of other life circumstances that people who work with people come across in their day-to-day employment.

It has also been used in the development and training of managers and organisations to enhance efficiency and solve often 'intractable' structural problems.

The approach is very different from more traditional 'problem focused' approaches. The focus away from problems and onto people's strengths and qualities which can be used in solution finding can be a challenge for some workers who have an existing body of formal and practice knowledge. The purpose of the introductory exercises is to validate what people find is effective in their current practice and relate this to some of the principles and practices of solution focused work, before moving onto using some of these in their work.

Solution focused work is in many ways a model of strengths based work (Milner *et al.* 2015). Dennis Saleebey was a key writer in this field and we suggest his work for further reading (Saleebey 2013). Strengths based approaches hold that people generally want to change their lives for the better and to play a constructive part in society through taking appropriate responsibility, and that they want to be respected and recognised for their contribution. These presumptions lead to practices that are optimistic and forward looking, as well as being brief and avoiding the creation of dependency. Solution focused approaches are part of this movement.

We now provide exercises to allow you to think in more strengths based ways. There are some for individual consideration and others that are for pairs and/or groups; we find that when working together the sum is often greater than the parts.

GOOD THINGS

Purpose: to practise strengths based interviewing; to identify your own strengths and good qualities

Using the table below write one good thing about yourself, with the attributes needed for this. The list can include any personal attributes – for example, skill at sport or art – both of which involve many attributes such as determination, concentration, patience, etc. Then consider how you can make more use of these attributes. Keep the list and add to it as you remember more personal qualities.

Good things about myself	Attributes	How can I use them more

SPARKLING MOMENTS

Purpose: to identify a person's qualities

This is an exercise developed by BRIEF (info@brief.org.uk), which in turn is based on ideas from narrative therapy (www.dulwichcentre.com.au).

- Think about the time when you were at your best, when you felt sparkling. Describe it briefly.

- What was that it in particular about that moment which caused it to stand out?

- What are you most pleased to remember about yourself at that moment?

- What else are you pleased to notice? What else? What else?

- If these qualities were to play an even bigger part in your life, who would be the first to notice?

- What would they see?

- What difference would that make?

INTRODUCTIONS AND BEST HOPES

Purpose: to introduce people to strengths based interviewing

Interview a colleague you do not know very well and find out who they are, what their job is, what makes them laugh, and what their best hopes are. Choose one quality they have described and explain to your colleague how this resonates with your experience.

Helpful questions for strengths interviewing

- What has made you smile today?

- What has happened today that has made life worth living?

- When did you recently feel uplifted by something?

- What is some small but really precious accomplishment you have achieved recently?

- What have you enjoyed recently that you have learned from? What do you do differently because of this?

- When have you appreciated your connection with another person?

- What was the last piece of work you did that you were proud of? How did you do this?

- What has been better about your work recently?

- In what ways have you been feeling more effective in your work recently? Which personal strengths did you use to achieve this?

- What specifically has gone right in your life recently?

- What has happened recently that has restored your faith in people?

IDENTIFYING SKILLS (ADAPTED FROM CHRIS IVESON, PERSONAL COMMUNICATION)

Purpose: to practise finding out what people can do well; to get feedback on a strengths based interview technique; to highlight the value of compliments

Ask two colleagues to join you in this exercise and take turns at being the interviewee, the interviewer and the interviewer's best friend.

- The interviewee has applied for a job, for which s/he has all the essential qualities.

- The interviewer is attempting to find out what marks this candidate out from the others (who are all level 'on paper') and how s/he handles difficult situations. The interviewer is *not* looking for deficits of any sort. The interviewer will take notes.

- The interviewer's best friend is observing the interview. As a best friend, this person will only notice what the interviewer does well. Again, notes are taken.

Stage 1
Conduct a ten minute interview. If you are short of questions, consult the prompt list below.

Stage 2
The interviewer feeds back what s/he has heard, commenting on what has impressed them, and why.

Stage 3
The interviewer's best friend feeds back on what impressed them about the interviewer, and why. (A variation is for the

best friend to write each skill or strength on a sticky note as they talk about it and then stick it on the interviewer, with permission and avoiding clothing that can be damaged!)

Stage 4

The interviewee gives feedback on how satisfied s/he was with the interview and is given the opportunity to say what questions s/he would have liked to be asked that would have elicited even more skills.

Question prompts

- When things go right, what do you do?

- What do you notice about other people when things go right?

- When you refuse to let things have a bad outcome, what do you do?

- What do you do to stop things getting worse?

- Which people are the most helpful to you? How do you use their help?

- When you feel you are doing something well, which once was difficult for you, what are you doing differently?

- What is the hardest thing you have ever done? How did you do it?

- What would your friends say are the best things they like about you?

- What is your proudest achievement? How did you do it?

OFF THE WALL QUESTIONS

Purpose: to practise developing creative questions

Judith once asked – via a translator – a large group of Italian counsellors and family therapists the question 'what is the hardest thing you have ever done?' There was some puzzlement initially and it soon became clear that the translator had said 'what is the oddest thing you have ever done?' This question worked just as well in identifying skills.

Draw up a list of off the wall questions and try them out on a colleague.

Extra skills prompts
These are useful for people who find it difficult to think of successes or good things about themselves, or who are used to being criticised:

- If you were in the diary room on *Big Brother* having to explain why you should not be ejected from the house, what reasons would you give?

- Consult the family dog. What would the dog say are the good things about you?

- Imagine you have a goldfish in your sitting room. It has got bored with swimming round the bowl and is amusing itself by studying you. What good things has it noticed about you that no one else has?

TOP TIPS: SKILLS RECOGNITION

1. When a member of your family or a colleague does something that impresses you, write it on a sticky note and place this on the fridge door or workplace noticeboard.

2. Join our 'Anti Tut Tut Club' – make a point of noticing when people do things well in ordinary life and bring this to their attention. For example, instead of tut tutting at parents of badly behaved children in public places, compliment the parents of well-behaved children, i.e. 'what a pleasure it is to see such delightful children. You must be doing something very right.'

Practice principles and assumptions

Many established ways of understanding people tend to focus on problems and the cause of them. This can include a strong belief that the difficulties people face are often the result of their childhood experiences: perhaps the way they were brought up or some adverse events in their formative years.

This can lead to a preoccupation with talking about the past and going over what has happened, in order to 'come to terms with' whatever trauma or problem the person has experienced. This is reinforced by our cultural expectations, where sayings such as 'you can't move on until you have dealt with the past' are common and frequently figure in popular media such as magazines. This is also common in some approaches to working with people, particularly psychodynamic approaches, although early psychoanalysts did not consider catharsis useful for all people (see, for example, Rycroft *et al.* 1966).

This focus on problems or deficits in people (something has gone wrong which has affected a person's normal emotional development) is also to be found in more modern therapies such as cognitive behavioural therapy, where people are seen to have 'distortions' in their thinking. These 'wrong' ways of thinking have developed due to people's experiences and environment, 'wiring' the brain in such a way that people have fixed and often unhelpful ways of processing and understanding information, leading to behaviours that can be damaging to themselves or others.

These people require 're-wiring', recognising that their existing responses to events are problematic and that they can learn other ways of behaving. This approach is quite common in working with violence, where people re-learn their automatic responses to certain events that trigger their anger, recognising the warning signs and replacing their aggression with other more reasonable behaviour.

The focus on problems (what is going wrong) and deficits (what is wrong with you) places the worker in a position of expert, diagnosing what the problem or deficit is and providing guidance on how to deal with this. It can lead to practice that reduces the opportunity for the person to be heard fully, replacing their stories with professional stories of what the problem is and how to deal with it. Kitwood (1997) refers to this as 'malignant psychology': things we do and say to people based on our theories of the nature of people that can have an incredible impact on them.

Many professionals use a checklist provided by their organisation to assess what level or type of service should be given to someone. These checklists are pre-formed with what are assumed to be relevant and important questions, and indeed they may be. However, the use of such checklists may lead to practice that only asks questions about the issues on the list and excludes what the person has to say about their situation if it does not appear on the schedule.

Solution focused practice rests on a totally different set of assumptions:

Assumptions about problems:

- The problem is the problem; the service user is not the problem.

- Problems do not necessarily indicate a personal deficit.

- Problems happen in interactions between people, rather than inside them.

- Problems are not always present; exceptions occur.

- Complicated problems do not always require a complicated solution.

Assumptions about the past:

- Events just happen; exploring the past leads to blame whereas the goal is to develop responsibility for the future.

- Exploring a problem-free future avoids having to dwell on or understand the past.

- A diagnosis does not have to determine the future.

Assumptions about change:

- Change always happens; nothing stays the same.

- What may appear to be small changes can be hugely significant.

- Change can be constructed through talk.

Assumptions about talking:

- Hearing what the service user has to say is important.

- Take a *not-knowing* stance that reduces premature and imposed worker judgment.

- Stay on the surface of conversations rather than looking beneath; any search for meaning is likely to be the worker's interpretation.

- People experience and make sense of the world in different ways; their reality may not be yours.

Assumptions about solutions:

- Identify what is going right rather than what is going wrong.

- Service users have the solutions to the problems; assist them in finding these.

- Solutions generated by the service user are more likely to be meaningful, achievable and successful.

- Imposing *what works* for others does not always work for the individual; seek what works for them.

- Increasing service user choices will enable behaviour change.

- Goals need to be meaningful for the service user in order to be successful, but they also need to be legal and moral.

The following exercises are designed to assist in understanding the differences between problem and solution focused practices, and to develop a more solution focused outlook. Consider the practice assumptions outlined above and how they are reflected in the exercises.

PROBLEMS TO SOLUTIONS

Purpose: to practise a solution focused approach to problems and remind yourself of interviews that went well

Problem Focused Questions	Solution Focused Questions
How can I help you?	How will you know when therapy has been successful?
Could you tell me about the problem?	What would you like to change?
Is the problem a symptom of something deeper?	Have we clarified the central issue on which you want to concentrate?
Can you tell me more about the problem?	Can we discover exceptions to the problem?
How are we to understand the problem in the light of the past?	What will the future look like without the problem?
How many sessions will be needed?	Have we achieved enough to end?

- In reflecting on the above lists, what differences can you see in the way in which the questions are phrased?

- What sort of questions do you use in your current practice?

- Which of your questions have been the most useful for the service users?

- Which of your questions have been most useful for you as a professional worker?

(From O'Connell 1998, p.21)

EVER APPRECIATING CIRCLES

Purpose: to allow people to notice the minutiae of competencies in their daily situations and to learn to look at the world with an appreciative eye rather than focusing on deficits

Stage 1

Look for things people do that you appreciate, particularly those hidden right in front of you. When you see them, acknowledge them verbally or nonverbally. Then pay attention to any evidence of an appreciative circle rippling back to you.

Questions:

- What do you notice at home that you appreciate?

- What do you notice about your colleagues and friends that you appreciate?

- Without people saying anything, in what ways do they make your day?

- What effect does it have on you?

- When you tell them what you appreciate about them, what difference do you notice about them physically, verbally?

- When you notice an appreciative circle rippling back to you, what difference does it make to you?

Stage 2

Select a family you work with where there is high criticism and low warmth. Ask them to begin looking at family members with an appreciative eye. Paul Hackett suggests that you can ask the family to acknowledge their appreciation by giving 'invisible badges' – a fingertip touch on the arm – and keep count of who gives and receives the most badges.

(From Paul Hackett 2005, p.83)

FROM PATHOLOGIES TO DESCRIPTIONS

Purpose: to help people who typically think in terms of diagnoses, deficits, dysfunction and pathology to begin to think in solution building terms and recognise that solutions do not necessarily need to be related to problems

Stage 1

In small groups, ask each participant to take the roles of client, therapist and observer. The client takes on the role of a diagnosis in the current DSM. They can choose their own diagnosis, e.g. ADHS, borderline personality disorder, depression, etc. They then read through the description of the diagnosis (readily available via Google). The therapist interviews the client about why they are in therapy and the client responds with the effects of the diagnosis and complaints about the difficulties they face with this disorder, including relationships. The therapist asks questions related to the problem. The diagnosis role is then passed to other members of the group and the process repeated.

Stage 2

The therapist then asks questions about how the aspects that are not related to the problem serve as strengths and support for the client, moving from general strengths and supports to specific ones. The therapist then asks the client to describe ways, times and supports that move from problem descriptions to non-problem descriptions – coping times, exceptions, etc. All questions must be built on the client's previous answers.

Stage 3

The client is asked to feed back to the group their experiences of each part of this exercise.

(From Nelson 2005, p.73)

SOLUTION FOCUSED SCAVENGER HUNT

Purpose: to practise identifying and using basic components of solution focused practice

Find a story about or an example of:

- a small change leading to a larger change

- a person's unique solution to a problem

- how looking ahead to a more positive future helped someone to change

- a time when a service user surprised you by recovering more quickly than you thought possible, or demonstrated strengths you didn't know they had

- doing something different that made a difference

- being part of someone's solution.

(From Fiske and Zalter 2005, p.127)

Practice principles

The nature of the relationship between workers and service users is the key to a successful intervention in someone's life. Being respectful of people, even when they may act in ways that are damaging or unhelpful for themselves or others, is important as it provides hope for the future and may well elicit new ways of behaving. Some people may be unused to being treated respectfully, or it may never have happened before, and they may expect to be told what to do, to be diagnosed or advised by a professional and be unable or constrained to take appropriate responsibility for their lives. Solution focused practice assumes that people are valuable and have the seeds of solutions within them, and that people have the propensity to be 'good' and to make positive contributions to life.

Empathy

Empathy is a concept that permeates much human service practice, based on the influential therapeutic ideas of Carl Rogers. We are told to be empathetic, and that we need to understand the feelings of another person in order to truly 'feel their pain' or situation. Terms such as 'walking in another's shoes' are commonplace, and have cultural weight in our psychotherapeutically influenced society. Solution focused approaches do not ignore emotions, nor do they dismiss them as irrelevant, but emotions are recognised as being understood and expressed in ways that are influenced by culture and the environment.

The expression of emotions is through actions, be they words, intonations, movements or other behaviours. Identifying emotional behaviours is important in solution focused practice because whilst people cannot help how they *feel*, they can change how they *behave*. For example, to say that someone 'loves' someone else is not enough in this construct, as it covers a range of meanings that are particular to the person and the situation. It is useful to ask questions about *how* someone loves another, changing the term from passive to active. Similarly it is not enough to ask a child to 'be good'; the 'good' behaviours that are expected need to be spelled out. The following exercises provide opportunities to consider how this works in practice.

TOP TIPS: GERUNDING!

Move a word from being a verb to being a noun (a *gerund*) so the conversation could, for example, be as follows:

> I love her!
>
> How do you do love?
>
> How does she know that you love her?
>
> What do you do that makes you a loving person?
>
> When are you at your loving best?
>
> What will you be doing when everyone can see that you love her?

FROM EMOTION TO BEHAVIOUR 1

Purpose: to identify how people 'do' emotions and what behaviours will affect emotions

This is a difficult exercise so ask colleagues, friends and family to help if needed.

Take the following words and try to identify the physical details of how you do these emotions (measurable behaviours):

Emotion	How it is done
Happiness	
Sadness	
Joy	
Misery	
Caring	
Concern for others	
Guilt	
Embarrassment	
Good self-esteem	

★

FROM EMOTION TO BEHAVIOUR 2

Purpose: to identify how people 'do' emotions and what behaviours will affect emotions

Take these words and try to identify how you do (measurable behaviours) these people skills:

Skill	How it is done
Empathy	
Listening	
Caring	
Non-judgmental	
Sympathy	
Understanding	
Helpful	
Useful	
Effective	

Validating emotions with a hint of possibilities (Rogers with a twist)

People can experience emotions that severely impact on their ability to deal with problems in their lives, and it would be insensitive not to acknowledge these. However, in solution focused practice the conversations are more than simply reflecting how someone describes their feelings. There is the opportunity to explore for potential strengths and exceptions to the apparently overwhelming negativity of the situation. When someone presents with a story of defeat, misery, damage and despair, then acknowledging this can be done without closing down the potential for change.

Question prompts

Consider the following responses to someone who has had a major adverse life event and is feeling overwhelmed:

- That must be scary/terrible/worrying [then add] *'at the moment'* or *'at this time'*.

- Have you ever felt…before? How did you recover *last time?*

- So, you've not been able to beat…*so far?*

- How have you stopped things getting worse?

- How are you managing to carry on *despite…?*

- But you still managed to get to the clinic – how did you find this determination?

Practice example: seeking exceptions

Therapist: Have you noticed any positive changes since we made this appointment?

Client: No. Nothing.

Therapist: Nothing at all?

Client: No. If anything, things have got worse...

Therapist: I see.

Client: Hmm. I can't control it *at all*!

Therapist: Can you explain a little more?

Client: Yeah. I've started vomiting after most meals.

Therapist: After most meals. I see...how come it's not after *every* meal?

(Jacob 2001, p.20)

Listening

Listening is viewed as a key skill in working with people. However, listening is not always straightforward and hearing what people have to say is influenced by the questions they are asked and our understanding of what people are saying.

We have a hurdle to overcome: the hurdle of wanting to make sense of what people say and fitting this into whatever framework we use to understand people. We have various theoretical understandings of people even though we may not always be aware of them, which influence when we decide we have truly heard the person.

Solution focused practice is wary of coming to a premature understanding of what people are saying, preferring to take a position of 'not knowing'. This stance is one of curiosity, trying to maintain an openness about the person by presuming that we do not know or we may be mistaken about what someone is trying to tell us.

Doing this enables us to ask further questions about the person and their situation that we may otherwise miss, thus reducing the opportunities to see complexity, meaning and solutions for the individual. As Turnell and Lipchik (1999) point out, it is the person's role to decide whether s/he is understood and it is the worker's role to build understanding of the person's description and experience of the problem, and their position on it. It is not the role of the worker to edit the person's account according to their own theories. Solution focused listening requires a genuine interest and a belief that there is no such thing as an ordinary person. The following exercises highlight some of the techniques used to enhance listening and communication.

TOP TIPS: LISTENING

Wait until you hear the answer to your question before framing your next question to make sure you are linking to what is being said to you.

CURIOUS QUESTIONING

**Purpose: to practise curious questioning and
increase listening skills**

With a colleague, think about the time you did the very best interview with someone in your job. Take it in turns to ask the person to say what they did. Then only ask the following questions of each other:

- How did you do that?

- What else?

- What else?

- What else?

- What else?

- Can you do more of it?

Carry on until you are exhausted or run out of answers!

COMMUNICATING CLEARLY

**Purpose: to ensure that the words you use
are understood and to help you avoid using
professional jargon**

Stage 1

In a small group, ask people to explain what these words
mean to them:

- responsibility

- respect

- consent

Stage 2

Ask people to identify 'professional' words and terms they
commonly use in reports (e.g. parallel planning, function,
prioritising the needs of children, risk, establishing
boundaries). The group then discusses exactly what they
mean by these words and terms and, where appropriate,
what specific behaviours illustrate these. Finally, ask the
group if they can think of simpler words they could use.

WORD WATCHING 1

Purpose: to develop listening skills; highlight the importance of checking that you have heard the person accurately; and practise suspending your hypotheses about problems

- Interview a colleague about any minor problem that person is experiencing.

- Listen carefully and feed back what you have heard using the exact words that the person used to describe their situation.

- Ask if you have 'got it right' and if there is anything they wish to change or amplify.

WORD WATCHING 2

Purpose: to remind yourself of the times you were able to see a person rather than a problem and highlight the importance of avoiding labelling

- Remember the last time a person came to you with a label (difficult, uncommunicative, bully, victim, etc.).

- How did you avoid seeing their label as the whole person?

- How did you find out about the times when they were not their label?

- How did you find out about their understanding of their label?

REFRAMING THE PROBLEM/DIAGNOSIS

Purpose: to provide an opportunity to practise solution focused talk and find people's unique ways of cooperating

Stage 1

Think of someone you are having difficulty in engaging and make a list of all the problem words you and others have used to describe this person. Then make a list of all the positive attributes this tells you about the person. For example:

Someone who is disrespectful, belligerent, uncooperative, disruptive, defiant, impossible, or has an attitude	may indicate that they are creative, have high energy, haven't given up or got depressed.
A person who is depressed	is possibly suffering from latent joy.
A person with borderline personality disorder	could be a person ready for change in direction.
Obsessive compulsive behaviour	means that the person is very good at attention to detail.

Stage 2

Think of the most uncooperative person you know. Remember a time when they cooperated (even if only slightly or with another person). What were you, or that person, doing that helped them to be cooperative?

If you can't find any time when they cooperated, ask them how you will be with them when they are able to cooperate with you.

Alternative

Undertake this exercise using an example of your child's lack of cooperation.

TOP TIPS: ENCOURAGING EXCEPTION FINDING

Double-sided report cards

For pupils who are on daily report for behaviour problems in class and conflict with teachers, re-design the report card to have two identical sides. At the bottom of one side write 'make a note of what [pupil's name] did well in your class'. On the other side write 'make a note of what [pupil's name] did wrong in your class but not until you have made a comment on the other side'. This alters the interaction between pupil and teacher with the latter being pushed into noticing good things about the pupil, or at least stopping them from looking out for negatives. The pupil is likely to change their behaviour to make the teacher say something positive about them.

Transparency

Solution focused work lends itself to transparency and openness in ways that other approaches often struggle to achieve. There is nothing hidden in a solution focused approach – no presumptions about the person or using preferred theoretical ways of analysing and understanding people. In professional roles people often find themselves baffled by jargon and questions that are laden with meaning that is not theirs. The following exercises provide the opportunity to consider how to be as open as possible, and therefore as respectful and empowering as possible.

TRANSPARENCY 1

Purpose: to practise being open about the extent and limits of your role; to highlight the importance of openness with service users; and to share with your service users your understanding of the nature of people and their problems

Stage 1
Conduct a first interview with a colleague as service user (you can use your latest referral details). Explain fully your role, what will happen to the information the person gives you, and outline the limits of confidentiality.

Stage 2
Explain briefly what method you use in your work. You can use any method for this part of the exercise, but do provide the service user with some understanding of the nature of your knowledge and how you understand people. This is important as service users often experience several different changes of worker and they are entitled to know in what ways they may approach problems differently.

TRANSPARENCY 2

Purpose: to demonstrate openness about what you heard and practise preparing solution focused feedback notes

Stage 1

Interview a colleague about a minor problem for ten minutes, and take notes which use their words. Then prepare feedback notes using these headings in the following framework:

- problem

- progress towards solving the problem (what they have done so far)

- solutions (how they did these things)

- next steps (what they have decided to do next to solve the problem and who will help).

Check the accuracy of the feedback notes with the person.

Stage 2

Repeat this exercise with the next person you see professionally. Take care to write down their description of the problem, not the professional one.

Practice example:
Recording sessions ▬▬▬▬▬▬▬▬▬▬▬▬▬▬▬▬▬

Session notes

Name: Micah

Date: 10 May 2016

Problem

Micah's biggest problem is daytime wetting. He has tried to stop it and gets so far but then it seems too hard and he gives up. Lots of things people have suggested to help have made him even more embarrassed, like the buzzer. He knows that he will have to solve it himself.

The pressure of being told off doesn't help. Micah gets told off a lot both at school and at home. Part of this is because he forgets things. Another thing which gets in the way of going to the toilet is being busy, watching television, arguing with his sister, doing his homework properly, and stuff like that.

Micah has two consciences, one bad and one good. The good conscience eggs him on to improve so that he can be like the other kids and not miserable at school. The bad conscience has been with him since he was seven and has got very strong. It tells him to ignore the good conscience, saying things like 'don't bother; life is not that bad, put up with it'. It also gets him to tell lies, steal, break things and be a bit rough and violent. He would like to get rid of the bad conscience.

Exceptions/progress

1. On Sunday Micah was dry for a whole day. He was pleased with his efforts and mum not saying 'oh, what's that smell?' and not having to go upstairs to change and missing his favourite television programme.

2. Sometimes Micah can go out with his mates and there is no wetting.

3. Sometimes he can recognise the feeling that he needs to go to the toilet. It is only a faint feeling. And he can hold on for five minutes.

4. He can remember to go to the toilet when he's doing something boring.

Thoughts on solutions

1. Micah did the whole day on Sunday because it was an enjoyable day. There was nothing bothering him, no pressure.

2. When he's out with his mates, Micah thinks that he's got to do it or there will be a wet patch and his mates will notice. He concentrates like mad but still enjoys himself. He would enjoy himself more and have a good feeling if he could be dry every day.

3. Micah can recognise the faint feeling best when he is relaxed, nothing troubling him. He is working on making this feeling stronger.

4. He can remember to go to the toilet when he's washing up and stuff like that.

Homework

The bad conscience has been living with Micah for so long it has got comfortable. It knows just how to wind him up and it can shut the good conscience up. So Micah will have to be a bit sneaky in how he gets rid of the bad conscience; this is what he may do:

He may do an experiment all week. He could toss the American coin each night. If it comes up on the building side, he would pretend all day that the good conscience has won – that he is not forgetful, that he can stay dry, and stuff like that. If it comes up heads he will have an ordinary day. His mum and dad have to see if they can notice any days are different from others but they won't know that he is tossing the coin.

To help keep the bad conscience from spoiling the experiment, Micah might carry a James Bond thing in his pocket. This might be James Bond cards or it might be something else.

If Micah has a better idea he will do this instead, or as well.

Afterthoughts

The worker, Judith, did think later that maybe the bad conscience is not as strong as Micah thinks. After all it couldn't stop him coming to counselling and having a good look at how it operates on him. Maybe the good conscience has been getting stronger in a quiet sort of way?

Child protection is often viewed as one of the most challenging areas of work. Solution focused approaches have been used to assist in being clear what the role, remit and concerns of professionals are, as well as enabling families to have their views heard. Safety underpins this work and it is possible to work in solution and strengths based ways whilst still having authority and professional and legal responsibilities.

TRANSPARENCY WITH CHILDREN
IN CHILD PROTECTION WORK

Purpose: to practise explaining your role to children and to highlight the importance of ensuring that children know the extent and limit of your power

Stage 1

With a colleague, using a child protection referral you are working on, draw a stickman picture which explains why you are visiting this family. This may include a drawing of a court or a case conference. Then draw a picture of the family events which have led to your visit.

Stage 2

Repeat this process with your real life service users. Check with the children that they have understood your drawings. Then ask them to draw a stickman picture of a happy and safe home.

(Adapted from Turnell and Essex 2006)

THE THREE HOUSES¹

Purpose: to assist children (or adults) to express their wishes and feelings

- Complete the three houses below about your current job.

- List what you are worried about; what is currently working well/OK; and what you would really like to achieve in the job.

- How might this activity be helpful with children?

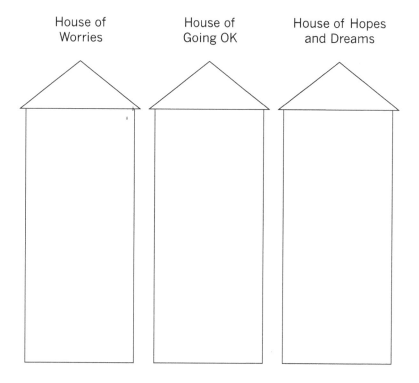

| House of Worries | House of Going OK | House of Hopes and Dreams |

---

1   Based on www.mythreehouses.com

TRANSPARENCY WITH ADULTS IN
CHILD PROTECTION WORK

Purpose: to practise developing cooperation and to demonstrate the importance of being clear about where your goals may differ from the family's

Using a child protection referral you are working on, in a group list all your and others' concerns on the left hand side of a flip chart. Then work out what the person will be doing differently when all these concerns no longer exist (this column should consist of demonstrable behaviours that can be evidenced and measured). Ask the people with other concerns to help you with this. Then consider what needs to happen for you to be happy to close the case. Lastly, work out a preliminary action plan.

Take care to avoid 'not' words, e.g. 'he will have stopped hitting', as this is not something that can be easily measured. Look for behaviours that demonstrate temper control, consideration, respect, etc. instead. Similarly where there are concerns about substance misuse, you might list: the rent arrears have been paid off, there is plenty of food in the fridge, the house is warm, etc. – all behaviours that show that money is not being spent on substances.

Practice example:
Being clear about safety

Donna has five children aged eleven years to three months to three fathers. The eldest four children are in foster care but see their mother and baby brother regularly at a hostel where her parenting is being assessed. The middle column shows Donna what she is already doing that contributes towards safety. The end column shows her what safety measures she needs to demonstrate for professionals to be happy for her to be reunited with her children.

Initial safety assessment: Amber, Thomas, Nisreen, Saqib and Tyler

Concerns	Evidence of safety	What safety will look like
1. Donna has a history of misusing cannabis and amphetamines, resulting in her children being allowed to play in the park on their own and her house getting into a very poor state	The tests Donna has undertaken show that she has been substance free for six months She attends a substance misuse prevention group	Donna will be continuing to provide test evidence that she is not misusing substances. Other evidence will be: a clean and tidy house, playing with the children rather than letting them go to the park on their own, doing reading practice with Amber and Thomas. Being on good terms with her family
2. Donna chooses the wrong sort of men as partners. Mark cheated on her and damaged the house when he was angry. Abdul was physically violent to her. Carlton drank heavily and was occasionally violent to her when drunk. Amber witnessed her mother being hit	Donna took out an injunction against Carlton and changed her telephone number so that she and the children were free of him After three bad choices, Donna now recognises that apologies and promises to change don't mean anything. She would rather live on her own at the moment	She will be living alone with the children, focusing on them and making sure that they are properly looked after She will be meeting new people as result of undertaking activities outside the home, e.g. attending college She will be on good terms with her family
3. Various professionals are concerned that Donna minimises the above concerns, acknowledging them at a superficial level only	Donna accepts responsibility for the behaviour which resulted in the children being removed from her care. She is reluctant to talk about it because: she is ashamed and embarrassed, but she knows what she did wrong and wants to find a solution so that she doesn't do these wrong things again	Remorse is easy to express and impossible to quantify. More measurable indicators of safety would be those listed at points 1 and 2
4. Donna suffers from depression and has self-harmed in the past	Donna has not self-harmed since the first threat to remove the children from her care. She consults her GP and takes her medication regularly. She is handling stress better these days	Donna will be confident and well. There will be no self-harming. She will ask for help when she has difficulties and be well supported socially

Children's goals	Parent's goals	Social Care's Goals
1. The children wish to return home to their mother	Donna wishes to get the children returned to her care, and a home	Donna to be substance free, doing the caring of the children, ensuring their safety, sticking to a routine, and cooperating with professionals
2. Amber wants her mum to stop smoking and give her dad a second chance	Donna wants an opportunity to prove that her behaviour has changed	Donna doing something for herself

2

Practice Principles and Techniques

Solution focused practice is comprised of several practice principles and techniques:

- There are always exceptions to problems, however small.

- Clear, measurable goals need to be established if the work is to be worthwhile.

- All people have strengths and qualities that can be used in finding a solution.

- Progress can be assessed by using scaling questions.

- It is important to assess whether the person needs assistance with increasing motivation, capacity or confidence to solve their problem.

The work is constantly evaluated to make sure we understand the person and are using their knowledge, not prescribing generalised programmes we have devised. There is no set format for a solution focused conversation other than starting with problem-free talk; the various techniques will be used in a fluid way so that they have meaning for the person. However, we separate the techniques here so as not to confuse. We start each section with a brief description of the technique, followed by practice examples and activities to enable the worker to practise the technique before using it in actual practice.

Beginning the conversation

How you start a solution focused conversation is important as most people will expect you to solve their problem, that is if they actually want to see you in the first place. Many people are 'sent' to be fixed by others. As a solution focused practitioner, it is your aim to get people to fix themselves by helping them view their problem from a different angle. Macdonald (2011) suggests the following opening questions:

- Hello, my name is…, what do you like to be called?

- What do you want to get out of coming here today?

- What will be different for you at the end of this session if it has been worthwhile for you?

- Can you tell me some good things about yourself?

Or you may prefer to begin with some problem-free talk. People are very used to talking about their problems and you can get so drawn into this that you forget to help them find their solution. Solution focused practice begins with problem-free talk: talk about what has been happening in their life just before your meeting. This is not just social chit chat as the solution focused practitioner is already on the lookout for strengths and resources.

CHALLENGING PROBLEM TALK

Purpose: to develop listening skills

Stage 1

Interview a colleague about his/her complaints about work for about five minutes. You may head nod but do not say anything. When the colleague has finished complaining, take a break and formulate a set of compliments based on what you have heard (these could be to do with their persistence, dedication, etc.). Deliver these compliments to your colleague.

Stage 2

Repeat this exercise with the next person you see professionally about a problem.

(From Ghul 2005, pp.63–4; Lamarre 2005, pp.65–6)

If this is a formal appointment, you might also look for any change that has happened since making the appointment and attending it. Very often the making of an appointment is sufficient to trigger some resolve to tackle the problem. Some people attend the appointment with the problem solved. For example, Katy requested counselling as she was very unhappy at home. She came for a brief informal chat to see if the service was for her and did a lot of thinking before she arrived for her appointment. Her initial goal of 'being happier' had developed into wanting to get more confidence in herself and not believing she was always in the wrong at home or had to keep doing things to please people. Therefore her first session consisted of a lot of questions about how she did that (for a fuller description, see Milner and O'Byrne 2002, pp.57–59). Other people want to talk about their problem and it can be very tempting to slip into 'expert' mode and offer some advice. It is important not to do this.

KEEPING SOLUTION FOCUSED

Purpose: to provide ideas for staying solution focused

The next time someone consults you about a problem (this can be a friend, colleague or anyone you're working with) do as follows:

- Think what advice you are going to offer but don't do this yet.

- Ask them what they have tried so far, what worked and what didn't.

- If something works a little bit, talk with them about how they can do more of it.

- If nothing worked, ask them what they could do differently.

- Ask if they have any resources for this.

- Discover what resources outside of themselves they need.

- And, if it has already been mentioned as something they tried and it didn't work, forget about the advice you are going to offer.

Asking questions about problems

The following is a list of helpful questions to enable the client to articulate their problem/s:

- How often does it [the problem] happen?

- How long has it been going on?

- Has it ever happened before?

- How did you deal with it then?

- What do people notice when it [the problem] is happening?

- What happens next?

- And then what?

- What else?

- If I were a fly on the wall, what would I see happening?

- Tell me about times when the problem is not so much a problem for you?

- What were you doing differently then?

The wonderful thing about these sorts of questions is that you will see the moment when the person stops sitting back and letting you do all the work and actually starts to think hard about what they can do differently, what choices they have and what strengths and qualities they can use, so it is important to go slowly and give the person time to think and process their ideas.

TOP TIPS: FOR CHILDREN AND YOUNG PEOPLE

1. Big Brother Diary Room

Where children are reluctant to talk, ask: if you were in the diary room, what would you be saying to the audience about your problem? What would you be saying that would make them vote to keep you in the house?

2. Customer complaints desk

Where families are talking over each other or children are being disruptive, nominate the most talkative person to staff a customer complaints desk and give them a pretend microphone. Explain that anyone can make a complaint about anything but once the customer complaints desk makes an official announcement on behalf of the complainant, everyone must help resolve the complaint. Alternatively, use a flip chart to record the discussion and possible solutions, and give the pen to the most talkative family member.

3. Football bench (from Couzens 1999)

Where group members are being disruptive, designate one member to be the umpire. If a member breaks a group rule (as established by the group), the umpire gives a warning. For a second breach of a rule, the member is sent to the 'sin bin' for a length of time decided on by the group. When they come back to the group, they apologise and the group talks about what sparked off the rule breaking. Should there be a third breach, the group member is asked to leave that group session and the behaviour is dealt with in an individual session.

4. Ask the audience

For children who lack ideas about solutions, ask them to consult with a friend or favourite character in a book or on television. What advice would this person give them?

Practice example: Talking with children

Tim has Asperger's syndrome and mild learning difficulties. He doesn't know what behaviour is appropriate (especially as he matures sexually), and is on the verge of being excluded from school for temper tantrums. On a temper taming scale (where one equals the worst temper ever and ten is completely calm), Tim rated himself five. He didn't know what he would be doing differently when he reached six on the temperature taming scale so Judith invited him to consult his helping team (Sally, his foster carer, and Anna, her granddaughter).

Tim: You mean like ask the audience?

Judith: Why not?

Tim: No, I'll phone a friend. [He puts his hand to his ear] You have to do it too, Judith.

Judith: Okay. [Putting her hand to her ear] Is that Sally? Hello. I have Tim here and he's answered all questions so far but he's stuck on this one: what would he be doing differently when he gets to six on the Temper Taming scale? You have 30 seconds, starting from now.

[Sally begins to answer but is distracted by Tim counting down the seconds loudly.]

Sally: I need a bit more time to think.

Tim: [Picking up Judith's mobile] We can use this.

Judith: Okay I'll ring you. [To Tim, pretending to use the mobile] Hello, is that Tim's teacher? I have Tim here and he's answered all questions so far but he stuck on this one: what would he be doing differently when he gets to six on the Temper Taming scale?

Tim: [as his teacher] He is a horror to work with. Let me see, he'll be sitting quietly not moving around, keeping calm and not walking out of class.

Judith: Thank you, that is most helpful. [Putting down the mobile and addressing Tim] Well, you heard what your teacher said. Do you think you can do any of those things?

Tim: Yes.

Judith: Which one will be the easiest one to start?

Tim: Not moving around.

Judith: How would you do this?

Tim: I knew you were going to ask me that! I'll just do it.

(Milner and Bateman 2011, pp.125–126)

Externalising the problem

This is a narrative therapy technique devised by White and Epston (1990) by which the problem is separated from the person so that people are not seen as problems. Having a diagnosis or being fitted into a category may be helpful in accessing resources but it has negative effects too in that workers then devise programmes for dealing with the diagnosis or categorisation rather than the person, assuming a one-size-fits-all approach. When the planned intervention fails to work, then the person is blamed and negative words are ascribed to him/her, such as resistant, in denial, unmotivated. This leads to the person being seen as the problem rather than as a person *with* a problem. No problem can adequately describe a whole person. Naming the problem also helps separate the person and problem so that all people concerned can then 'gang up' on the problem rather than the person. Externalising problems removes blame from the situation, freeing people up to be creative about how they deal with problems.

Practice example:
Externalising in practice
Writing about living with early onset dementia, Kate Swaffer says:

> If you think of dementia as we do in my house, and that 'it' is the third person in a threesome, it could be seen as both of us living with 'it'. And we call this troublesome threesome the Three Stooges, and have even named 'it', Larry! (2015, p.202)

INDIVIDUALISING THE PROBLEM

Purpose: to get a clear and detailed description of a problem; avoid jumping to a hasty assessment of what the problem is; and provide an opportunity to begin externalising the problem

In small groups, ask people to describe an emotion (e.g. anger, upset, frustration) using the following questions:

- What colour is it?

- What shape is it?

- Where in your body does it live (e.g. head, stomach, chest)?

- What is the first sign that it is about to start?

- Where in your body does it go next?

- What does it get you to do?

- How long does it last?

- What do other people notice?

- When it has gone, how do you feel about yourself?

- How do you calm yourself?

- What else?

- Can you do more of this?

You can have a lot of fun with this exercise, listing answers on a flip chart. For example, if you are looking at temper, you can divide the answers into colours (not always red) and then draw the shapes which are often explosive, although sometimes implosive. Comparing how people calm themselves not only gives other group members more ideas but also shows how very diverse emotional expression is. At the end of this exercise, you will probably have a list of names for temper, not all of which will be red mist or red bomb by any means.

Children are more likely than adults to decide on a name for their problem. Where adults find it harder to see the problem as external – for example, 'I'm an addict' (or more likely to be expressed as 'I'm a smack head') or 'I'm an anorectic' – you can simply use a more straightforward, less negative problem name. In the examples here, you could hold an externalising conversation with heroin or food as the problem, in which you interrogate the problem not the person.

Problem interrogating questions

- Is heroin for you or against you?

- How did heroin con you into thinking that you need it in your life?

- What influence does heroin have on your life, on those close to you, and your relationships?

- Given a choice between heroin and life free of heroin, which do you choose?

- What prevented you from resisting heroin? How did heroin use these things to move into your life?

- How much of your life will heroin be satisfied with, or does it want the lot?

- Does it suit you to be dominated by heroin?

- Tell me about a time when you didn't fall for the lies heroin has been telling you.

- Tell me about a time when you made heroin wait.

- What does it say about you as a person when you refuse to cooperate with heroin's invitations?

- In the times when you have felt in control of heroin, what are the things that helped you have that control?

- Tell me about a time when heroin didn't stop you being in touch with your hopes and dreams.

You will see that the questions are developing from an interrogation of heroin to those looking for exceptions and strengths which will form part of the solution.

Exceptions

De Shazer discovered the importance of exceptions when talking with a man who complained of always being depressed. De Shazer asked him how he knew he was depressed if it happened all the time to which the man answered that he knew he was depressed because sometimes it wasn't quite as bad. De Shazer then asked him what he was doing differently during these times when it wasn't so bad, as these exceptions hold the seeds of a solution. Exceptions can be very small but this doesn't matter as they can be grown. Like making a snowman, the hardest part is getting the central core established; it rolls on quickly once you have got started. Many people discount exceptions (it just happened) or say there aren't any (I can't help it). It is very rare for there to be no exceptions but you may have to work hard to discover them.

Practice example: Exception findings

Jack could think of only one time when he could have responded violently to a situation but he didn't: 'Me brother...last night he wound me up and I wanted to smack him. I said "shut up, you're winding me up" and walked out'. When asked how he did this, he replied, 'Well, it weren't my flat. If it had been my own flat, I'd have hit him.' Although minuscule in terms of temper control, it was an important exception from which to begin building responsibility-taking, because it had meaning to his life.

(Milner and Jessop 2003)

EXCEPTION FINDING

Purpose: to find out when problems are less of a problem

- Choose a behaviour with some compulsion that you would like to change such as overeating, shopping, smoking.

- Think of a time when you were able to resist the compulsion and analyse what you were doing differently at this time.

- Or think of a time when things were going more smoothly than usual. What was different about that time?

Question prompts for exception finding

- Tell me about the times you are *not*...

- Tell me about the times you are *less*...

- Tell me about the times you can cope *despite* this feeling...

- When you feel like...and you don't, what do you do?

- How did you do that?

- Tell me about the time you refused to let...ruin your day.

- When was the last time that you stopped...from spoiling your day?

- What will it be like when [the exception] is happening more?

- Who will notice when [the exception] is happening more?

- Who could help you do it [the exception] more?

Where people have difficulty in identifying any exceptions to their problem you can set them tasks.

Pretend tasks

Pretend tasks are helpful for generating exceptions where the person is having difficulty in seeing any. When people pretend to be less depressed they are likely to have a better week and be able to report some small changes. Is there any difference between pretending to be less depressed and being less depressed? Certainly others often cannot tell the difference and react with the person accordingly. Pretending is virtually the same as doing it and shows that one can; de Shazer says that pretending:

> serves to disconnect the solution construction and development process from the problem and to bypass the client's historical, structural perspective and any disagreements about what the problem is. Once a solution develops... It no longer matters what the problem might have been. (1991, p.114)

Berg and Reuss (1998) suggest that a coin toss is added to the task, for example, for women who cannot make a decision whether or not to leave an alcohol-addicted partner – the supposedly co-dependent woman. The coin determines on a particular day whether someone is pretending that no matter how good the situation gets she will leave her partner or no matter how bad the situation gets she will stay with him or her. This gives her space to see how either decision would feel. We elaborate even further when using pretend tasks in order to address in a very small way feelings of powerlessness. We like to build up a story around the coin, asking the person to choose from a selection of foreign coins which one represents the place they would most like to visit when the problem is no longer there. When the pretend task is to have one day pretending – depending on the toss of the coin – that all their problems are solved, or have an ordinary day, we also ask them to choose which side of the coin is the happiest side and nominate this as the problem-solved pretend day.

For people who say that they find it difficult to pretend that their problems are solved, we combine the task with 'borrowing from a life they admire'. For example, Lindsay wanted to 'be better' at school but didn't want to be seen as a 'swot' on her pretend days. She identified another pupil who managed to combine 'being good' with being popular so Lindsay's task was to pretend to be this girl on happy coin side days (Milner and O'Byrne 2002, p.53). What we most enjoy about this experiment is the number of times the coin seems to turn up on the favoured pretend days. Where there are relationship problems or complaints about behaviour, the complained-about person can be asked to pretend to be better some days and the complaining person asked to discern which days. This undermines a problem story as well as empowering the complained-about person to behave differently without losing face.

Prediction tasks

Prediction tasks are often used to develop some control over difficulties that seem to be beyond the person's control, for example, hearing voices or having an urge to do something antisocial. People who practise predicting compulsiveness can get more and more of their predictions right; when they get most right we have proof of some control. For example, David worried about drinking bouts that led to violence but could not identify any control other than it depending on what mood he was in when he got up. He was given a prediction chart and asked to consult his parents and girlfriend to see if they could predict good days and what they noticed was different about him on those days. At his next appointment he reported that he had predicted a bad day and worked out with his girlfriend how to handle it differently. In another example, Kylie had a large file at her children's home filled with details of misbehaviour. She was asked to undertake a pretend task but also tell staff that she was doing a good and bad behaviour experiment and ask them if they could predict which days were likely to be which. This changed how they reacted with her (Milner and O'Byrne 2002, p.54).

There is no expectation that the task will be undertaken; it is a means by which a person can start to look for solutions, notice them and have them noticed (see the practice example of Micah earlier). Often people have better ideas of their own.

DEVISING A TASK

Purpose: to practise creating prediction tasks

This is an exercise for the worker to practise.

1. Think about or discuss what in your present life you want to keep the same.

2. You have several good ideas already for reaching your goals. We think that you should do more of what you are already doing.

3. You have tried many ideas already with limited results. It is time to try something completely new. You will know best yourselves what to try after you have thought about it.

4. Each evening predict where you will be on the scale tomorrow and check next evening if you were right.

5. Pretend on one day each week that the miracle has happened but do not tell anyone which day you have chosen.

(From MacDonald 2011, p.28)

Strengths

Solution focused approaches are concerned with finding the strengths that people have, even when they may either not recognise them as such or have minimised them. We often find that people are reluctant to admit that they have strengths and are much more comfortable talking about problems or deficits. This is to be avoided, as it generates feelings of helplessness and despair that are not very helpful in constructing positive solutions, even though some people may actually enjoy relating tales of misery. Some people are brought up to believe that saying that you are good at something is boastful, or they may have been undermined when younger through severe criticism, therefore learning to avoid any acknowledgement that they can be competent, creative and have real strengths and successes. Sometimes strengths are well hidden, but they can also be staring us in the face – we just haven't seen them for what they are. The solution focused practitioner can assist in encouraging the person to recognise their strengths, even when they may be doubted, dismissed or denied.

FOCUSING ON STRENGTHS

Purpose: to practise looking for strengths rather than deficits

Simon was a young man who had experienced major adversities in his life, having being rejected by his parents at an early age and subsequently placed in a bewildering range of unsuccessful foster placements. Now 17, he was lonely, miserable, struggling to make friends and self-harming, with little sense of how he could change his life. He was referred to a specialist project for isolated young people and was seen by James, a worker who had trained in attachment theory. After listening to Simon describe his problems and feelings, James shared with Simon that he thought that his problems stemmed from the difficulties of his childhood which had created ways of being that were deep rooted, and that his training and experience led him to believe that Simon could resolve his problems but that it would take at least two years of weekly therapy exploring his past to achieve this. Simon appreciated the help offered but found it difficult to imagine committing to such a long-term project and became preoccupied with his past experiences. His self-harming became more pronounced.

Make a list of the strengths and resources that you think Simon has. Then prepare a list of questions that will elicit more strengths and abilities.

SUCCESS AND FAILURE

Purpose: to invite people to consider the role of emotions in the way we tell stories; allow them to recognise the importance of focusing on strengths; and experience the consequences of focusing on problems

Stage 1

Think of a time when you succeeded in a difficult task. With a colleague, discuss what immediate feelings accompanied the success. What sort of self-talk did these feelings provoke?

Stage 2

Think of a time when you failed something small. With your colleague, discuss what immediate feelings accompanied the failure. What sort of self-talk did these feelings provoke?

(Adapted from Young 2005, p.85)

Practice example:
Eliciting strengths

Marie visited Jane, who had been diagnosed with depression and there were concerns about her care of the children. Jane appeared to be very unhappy and the home was dark with the curtains drawn even during the day. Jane expressed her misery at the situation and her sense of failure as a parent. Marie heard this then asked Jane to tell her about the things that she and her children were good at. Jane was a little perplexed at first, but was able to list a whole series of strengths and achievements of her children, then began to recognise that she was responsible for these.

Marie asked more questions about how Jane had encouraged such positives in her children despite the depression. Jane was able to move to talking about herself and the qualities she had as a parent. Far from being a preliminary social chit-chat, the conversation developed from the first as a tool to assist Jane in thinking about how she could deal with the constraining effects of depression using her temporarily hidden strengths. The talk was good humoured as Jane was invited to identify those times when her child had made her proud, including the things that made her laugh. At the end of the session Jane was in a much better frame of mind to work with Marie towards solutions. As Marie left, Jane opened the curtains and let in the light.

Additional questions for eliciting strengths:

- I know very little about you apart from what brings you here. What would you feel happy to tell me about yourself?

- What are you interested in?

- What do you enjoy?

- What are you good at?

- [For relatives] What does [service user] do that makes you proud of him/her?

SEARCHING FOR STRENGTHS

Purpose: to practise focusing on what people can do well and develop a range of questions which elicit strengths

Consider the list of previous questions.

- What other questions might you ask in this manner?

- How would you answer these questions?

- What feelings do these questions generate in you?

ELICITING SKILLS

Purpose: to help you identify your existing skills

Think of a professional intervention you had with someone that had a positive outcome for the service user.

- How did you both agree about the nature of the problem?

- How clear were you with them about your perception of the problem?

- How did you both agree about when the intervention should end?

- How did you plan for the ending?

- In retrospect, could you have ended the work sooner with a reasonable outcome?

- If so, how?

TOP TIPS: ELICITING STRENGTHS OF VULNERABLE PEOPLE

Defiant children

Defiant children are not particularly bothered about praise. Indeed, if you tell a defiant child that something they have done pleases you, you have just given them another means by which to annoy you when they do the opposite. Equally, they will tend to dismiss your indirect compliments as defiant children often have high levels of self-esteem. Instead you can compliment by 'noticing'; for example you can say in an almost disinterested way, 'I noticed that you were kind to your little sister' and then leave it at that until there is another 'noticing' opportunity. In their book *Try and Make Me!,* Levy and O'Hanlon (2001) recommend that you deliver ten acknowledgements for every single negative comment you make to a defiant child so they begin to notice what they're doing really well.

People with dementia

Baker (2015) explains explain how to identify a person's strength even when they have considerable cognitive impairments. These strengths can then be used to help the resident feel more valued and be more settled in residential care, for example. She says:

> I remember a headmistress in one of our homes constantly told the other residents off, telling them to behave and to sit down and be quiet as she believed she was still in her role within the school, and the residents before her were her children. Because we knew this about this particular lady, we

were able to work alongside her and guide her into other activities that occupied her frame of reference at that time, encouraging her to look at 'registers', at the diary or at some books. This helped her to feel she was doing something of value, which ultimately maintained her well-being and self-esteem, and reduced the risk of distressing other residents within the care home. (pp.50–51)

ELICITING STRENGTHS 1

Purpose: to practise identifying strengths in difficult situations

- Think of a child you find challenging to work with now.

- Now think of three good things about this child.

- What difference will recognising these good things make to your work with the child?

- Does the child know these good things about themselves?

- What questions can you ask the child that will reveal the things about them?

ELICITING STRENGTHS 2

Purpose: to practise identifying strengths in difficult situations

- Think of a resident in your home whose behaviour is trying to both staff and other residents.

- Look back at his/her history, discussing with relatives if necessary to find out what this person's strengths have been throughout their life.

- Then discuss in the staff group how these strengths can be used to improve the situation for both that person and the home.

Developing goals

It is important to have clear goals as otherwise you will have no way of knowing whether or not your work has been effective. A simple way of doing this is by asking:

- How will you know that meeting with me will be worthwhile?

- What will you notice?

- What are your best hopes?

- What will need to happen for you to know that our work is helpful to you?

- What will other people notice?

It is easier to measure whether or not goals have been achieved if you have defined them in clear, concrete behavioural changes; for example, 'I will be happy' is a broad goal that needs to be developed by asking the person what they will be doing differently when they are happy. You can ask: 'Suppose I looked through a window into your house and could see that you are happy. What would I see, what would you be doing? What does happiness look like?' This helps to ensure that there are no misunderstandings or misinterpretations by the worker of what happiness means to that person. It also helps the person talk through what they will be actually doing when their best hopes are achieved, increasing their personal responsibility-taking. This breakdown will make the goals appear small and achievable in contrast to one large overarching goal, which at the beginning of the work can feel unreachable and overwhelming. This doesn't mean that your goals will always be modest ones. It simply means that you will start out with the simplest, most easily achievable goal.

People have a tendency to describe goals negatively, such as 'He won't be hitting anyone' or 'I won't be using heroin'. Again, it is easier to measure whether or not you have been effective if your goals are framed in terms of the presence or start of something rather than absence or end of something. Goals do change and develop further over time but must always be ethical, achievable, time limited and measurable, otherwise you don't really know what you are doing.

DEVELOPING CLEAR GOALS

Purpose: to begin looking at measurable outcomes

- Think of a person with whom you are working whose referrers describe the problem in negative terms.

- What will this person be doing differently that will convince the complainers that the problem is no longer present?

More questions to aid goal setting

- What sort of person do you want to be?

- What can you see yourself doing when you will be doing [the goal], right here today?

- What will people notice that will be different when you are doing [the goal]?

- How might they respond differently to you?

- How do you think this will be helpful to you?

- When will be the first opportunity to do [the goal]?

- How will you know when you don't need to come here any more?

- How will I know that you don't need to come here any more?

GOAL SETTING WITH PEOPLE WHO ARE VIOLENT TO THEIR PARTNERS

Ask the violent person to complete the following 'Overcoming Violence Scale' chart and the non-violent partner to complete it with their views on how they think the violent partner would answer. Compare the two charts and note areas of agreement. Then ask the non-violent person to select the one item they have scored as 'not at all' or 'just a little' which would make a big difference if it was one point higher. This becomes the goal for the violent person.

Overcoming Violence Scale

No.	Tick the box that fits best	Not at all	Just a little	Pretty much	Very much
1	I can talk calmly when I argue				
2	I can listen to my partner without interrupting				
3	I have a method to ensure we take turns				
4	I can accept that s/he has a right to be upset				
5	I feel appreciated and cared for by my partner				
6	When s/he is upset, I wait for her/him to calm down				
7	I do not use 'put-downs'				
8	If s/he puts me down, I have a planned response				
9	We respect each other's opinions				
10	We trust each other				
11	I can resist using sarcasm in arguments				
12	We can be honest with each other without fear				
13	When I notice angry words starting I have a plan to prevent them				

★

No.	Tick the box that fits best	Not at all	Just a little	Pretty much	Very much
14	I remember it is okay to *feel* angry but not okay to *do* anger, including words				
15	I take responsibility for the harm I have done using violence				
16	I realise I have no right to use violence to get my own way				
17	I do not feel I need to win when I argue with my partner				
18	I have worked out where my attitudes and ideas that say violence is okay have come from				
19	I can challenge attitudes and words that support violence				
20	When we argue we are not afraid of either one of us losing control				
21	I have ways to make it easier for my partner to tell me what she thinks				
22	I have ways of handling frustration at work				
23	I can control my drinking				
24	I can resist taking drugs				
25	I can ask for what I want politely (not expecting mind-reading)				
26	I ask for help when I need it				
27	We regularly plan things to promote a violence-free relationship				
28					
29					

The 'miracle question' for goal setting

This helps people focus on what life will be like when the problem is more manageable or has been resolved. It goes like this:

> Now, I want to ask you a strange question. *Suppose* that while you are sleeping tonight and the entire house is quiet, a *miracle* happens. The miracle is that *the problem which brought you here is solved.* However, because you are sleeping, you don't know that *the miracle has happened.* So, when you wake up tomorrow morning, *what will be different* that will tell you that a miracle has happened and the problem which brought you here is solved?

FOLLOW UP QUESTIONS TO THE MIRACLE QUESTION

- What will you notice? What else, what else, what else?

- What will you see?

- What will be different?

- What will other people notice about you?

- Picture later in the morning; what is happening now? What else is telling you the miracle has happened?

- And at work/home/other places, what is different here?

- And back at home, late afternoon, what do you notice now?

- What sort of things are you saying to yourself at the end of the day?

The 'nightmare question' for goal setting

Reuss (Berg and Reuss 1998) created a nightmare question for people who are very pessimistic about their future, such as problem drinkers for whom quitting is not a solution but just one more problem:

> Suppose that when you go to bed tonight a nightmare occurs. In this nightmare all the problems that brought you here suddenly get as bad as they can possibly get… But this nightmare comes true. What would you notice tomorrow that would let you know you were living a nightmare life?

FOLLOW UP QUESTIONS TO THE NIGHTMARE QUESTION
First explore the details of the nightmare with the same questions as for the miracle question. Then:

- Are there times now when small pieces of the nightmare are happening?

- What is the nightmare like during those times?

- Who is most affected by the nightmare when it happens?

- Who is most interested in seeing that the nightmare is prevented?

- What would it take to prevent this nightmare from happening?

- How confident are you that you can do what it will take?

It is possible that a couple may have different nightmares so more questions are needed:

- When she is living her nightmare and you are living yours, what will you notice about each other?

- How will these nightmares destroy what you have both been working for?

The nightmare scenario is only used when all other questions have failed to be effective and is a last ditch attempt to keep going with what seems a hopeless situation. In effect, it helps the person *imagine* hitting rock bottom rather than actually doing so.

THE MIRACLE QUESTION

Purpose: to practise the miracle question

As a worker you know that you sometimes struggle to complete the required agency forms on time. This causes you anxiety, especially when you and your supervisor are under pressure due to frequent inspections. Imagine that tonight you go home, have dinner and relax, then go to bed as usual. During the night something miraculous happens, and the problems you have in completing the forms disappear completely. Because you are asleep you do not know that this is the case.

- When you go to work in the morning, what will be the first thing you notice that will tell you that the miracle has happened?

- What will your colleagues notice that is different?

- What will your supervisor notice that is different?

- What will you be doing differently?

However, many seemingly 'unrealistic' answers are not unrealistic at all; they may well result from what Hawkes, Marsh and Wilgosh (1998) describe as the 'poverty of choice' of people who are suicidal or psychotic: thinking that there is only one solution. They give the example of a person wanting to line his room with tinfoil to block out radio waves that plague him. They suggest that this man has a goal of wanting to achieve peace and quiet and that there are other ways of reaching this reasonable goal: wearing a helmet, playing music louder, taking medication, learning to ignore voices, talking to someone, staying with relatives, moving bedrooms, and so on:

> [A]lthough the means may often be illogical, eccentric or crazy (tinfoil, wearing a helmet) the end is often understandable, valid and sane (peace and quiet, sleep). We all want peace and to feel safe, to trust others, etc. We don't all achieve this by hiding away, wearing a loin cloth or lining our rooms with tinfoil. If you look beyond the client's attempted solution, the end they desire is often salient, understandable and sane. (Hawkes *et al.* 1999, p.91)

People who are used to having their problems diagnosed and remedies prescribed are highly likely to say they don't know the answers to the miracle question so it is important to go slowly and patiently.

Practice example:
The miracle question

Therapist: What will be the first thing you notice that is different as you open your eyes?

Client: I don't know... [Therapist waits patiently]

Client: You ask weird questions!

Therapist: I do, you're right... [Continues to wait]

Client: I suppose I'd not wake up thinking about food.

Therapist: Hmmm?

Client: Can't think of anything else.

Therapist: Okay. So... If you're not thinking about food, what else would you be thinking about?

Client: Now, that I *really* don't know!

Therapist: Another tricky question! [laughter]

Client: Hmmm. What would I be doing instead? I suppose about what I'd be doing that day.

Therapist: Is it a working day or a weekend day?

Client: Definitely a weekend.

Therapist: So there you are, in your bed, it's the weekend... Just opened your eyes thinking, what shall I do today?

Client: Hmmm.

Therapist: How do you feel?

Client: I wouldn't feel so down and depressed.

Therapist: Oh, okay. So how *do* you feel?

Client: Dunno, really... I feel happy... And relaxed.

Therapist: Imagine you could watch this scene on video... Can you describe to me what you see yourself doing differently? How do you *see* that you are happy and relaxed?

Client: I'd be snuggled up, with a smile on my face. Yeah. And... And I probably think, I'll ring one of my friends and go to the beach.

Therapist: Good idea! Is it a sunny day?

Client: Too right it is! Yeah, lovely. A day by the beach.

Therapist: So then what happens? Do you jump out of bed? Do you snuggle down a little longer?

Client: No I'll jump out. [Shows jumping action with hand]

Therapist: Full of bounce!

Client: Yeah, full of energy.

Therapist: And then what will you do differently on this miracle day?

Client: I'll have a shower.

Therapist: And what's different about that?

Client: I won't be pinching and punching my stomach...

Therapist: What you do instead?

Client: I can stand under the shower for ages and...

Therapist: And... What else?

Client: And I really like my body. I can bear to look in the mirror. I will have lost some weight.

Therapist: Mmm! And then?

Client: Yeah. Then I'll get dressed and have some breakfast.

Therapist: Do you choose anything different to wear?

Client: Yes. I won't wear drab or black.

Therapist: Okay, so instead what will you choose?

Client: Some bright colours, my shocking pink T-shirt.

Therapist: Aha! To match your hair! [Client has bright pink streak in her hair]

Client: [laughs] Yeah! Cool!

Therapist: Okay. And then, you say you have breakfast. What would you have on this Miracle day?

Client: I won't have rubbish.

Therapist: So what will you go for?

Client: Hmmm... Some cereal.

Therapist: Anything else? Miracle day remember? A special treat perhaps?

Client: Oh yes! I'll treat myself to some of that nice expensive orange juice with bits in.

Therapist: You make my mouth water!

Client: And mine! [Laughter]

Therapist and client continue to explore the miracle day in detail. (Jacob 2001, pp.22–23)

QUESTION PROMPTS FOR 'DON'T KNOW' ANSWERS TO 'HOW DID YOU DO IT?

- Look puzzled and wait.

- It's a difficult question...

- Maybe you know and don't know at the same time, that's hard to say...

- Take your time and think about it, there's no rush.

- Guess.

- Suppose you did know, what would the answer be?

- Perhaps I've not asked this question in a helpful way; how could I ask it better?

- What advice would you give to a person with a similar problem to you?

- (For small children) Oh, I see. It's a secret. Okay.

- Perhaps you might like to study what happens next time and see if you can spot how you did it?

- Okay, so what would [name of loved one] say about it?

MIRACLE QUESTION WHERE THERE ARE CONFLICTING GOALS

Give each family or group member a piece of paper and a pen. Ask them to write down their answer to the miracle question and keep their answer hidden. Then ask one member what s/he thinks another member has written and so on until each person has guessed what another has written. Choose who guesses which answer according to your knowledge of the group so no one is threatened by the process. Then ask each person if the guesses were right or wrong. The ensuing discussion of difference will lead to the group deciding on a first goal for all or prioritising one person's goal.

TOP TIPS: GOAL SETTING WITH PEOPLE WITH LEARNING DIFFICULTIES

1. Social stories

Begin a story about the person, outlining how the problem is affecting them and then ask the person what happens next. Where the story goes in the direction which is failing to deal with the problem, add a paragraph on consequences and then ask again, 'What happens next?' Where the story goes in the direction of solutions, you ask, 'How did you do that? What else? Can you do that again?' You can write the story down or draw pictures for the person to take away for reference. Remember to break the goal down into small, easily understandable pieces.

2. Can-Do Dinosaurs[1]

These consist of a pack of 24 friendly monster cards specially designed to reinforce learning about safety; for example *I Can Say No*, *I Can Tell Others*, *I Can Ask for Help* and *I Can Keep Safe*.

3. Mr. Men characters

These are useful for people with limited conceptual and drawing skills as they are simple to draw and only address one behaviour at a time. The first Mr or Miss is

---

1   See http://innovativeresources.org/resources/card-sets/can-do-dinosaurs/

the problem, for example, Mr Cheeky, or Miss Temper. Then ask the person to draw a second character which is the solution, for example, Mr Polite or Miss Calm. Follow-up questions would include, 'Tell me about a time Mr Cheeky tried to get you into trouble but failed', and 'Tell me about a time when Miss Calm came out'.

QUESTION PROMPTS FOR EXTREME PESSIMISM OR LACK OF A CLEAR GOAL

- How will you know when you don't need any help any more?

- Most problems have advantages as well as disadvantages. How can we keep the advantages at the same time as we get rid of the disadvantages?

QUESTION PROMPTS TO AID GOAL SETTING

Goals need to be specific, 'doable' and measurable, consisting of doing something rather than the absence of something.

- What sort of person do you want to be?

- What can you see yourself doing when you will be doing your goal, right here today?

- What will people notice that will be different when you are doing this goal?

- How might they respond differently to you?

- How do you think this will be helpful to you?

- When will be the first opportunity to do your goal?

- How will you know when you don't need to come here any more?

- How will I know that you don't need to come here any more?

TOP TIPS: GOAL SETTING WITH CHILDREN

1. Back to the future

Invite the child or young person to join you in a time machine (choose one from a topical television programme). Then say: 'When you open the door, you are outside your house in...years' time' [choose a time span appropriate to the age of the child and linked to a life transition, such as starting secondary school]. You look through the window and you can see yourself inside. My word, it is clear that you don't have a care in the world; what a success you have made of your life.' Then elicit a detailed description of this life by asking:

- What are doing?

- Which room are you in?

- Where is this house?

- What is the furniture like?

- What colour are the walls, etc.?

- Are there any other people with you?

- What are they doing?

- What pictures, photos are there?

- Whose numbers are in your mobile?

- What else, what else?

Then say: 'You are so amazed at how well you have done that your nose is pressed against the window and s/he has seen you. S/he invites you in and you say: 'How *did* you do it?' Then continue with a solution focused conversation.

Most children can answer this question immediately because they have now been talking about their older, competent self at some length. For those children who struggle to answer the question, they can be invited to ask their older, wiser self for advice or comfort: 'Okay, so you can't tell me *yet*, but can you tell me how you got through this difficult time?' This invites the child to work out what would be comforting during the current difficulties. Additionally, because you added the word 'yet' in this question, you are presupposing that the child will be able to answer the question at some time in the future.

2. Cartooning

Here a large sheet of paper is divided into six squares and the child is invited to draw the problem in the first square, how they would rather be in the second, a 'mighty helper' in the third, what a slip back might look like in the fourth, how it is handled in the fifth, and how success will be celebrated in the sixth (from Berg and Steiner 2003).

TOP TIPS: FOR ADULTS 1
Consulting a wiser older self

Ask the person to choose a friend who they see sporadically and then ask them to write a letter from the future. This letter begins with, 'You will be pleased to hear that my problem is no more and I'm very happy. I'm...'. You then ask the person the same questions as listed above for Back to Future. Then you suggest to the person that the recipient of the letter will want to know how they did it, so they can then follow up with the details of the solution.

The miracle question

Elaine, a 17-year-old who was accommodated and in supported lodgings, was referred by her social worker for assistance with depression and self-harming behaviours resulting from earlier emotional and physical abuse. Elaine was unhappy with her lodgings which were socially isolated, found her social worker unhelpful, had no family or friends, no hobbies, little interest in the future, no motivation, and was overweight, drinking and in debt. Life had been so hard for Elaine that she couldn't formulate even the simplest goal so she was asked about cherished dreams in an adapted version of a 'letter from the future'.

She was asked to say exactly what she would be doing if her wildest dream came true. She thought this rather silly but made a start, helped by asking questions and enjoying the dream with her: she would be sitting beside a swimming pool, drinking a mint julep. The pool would be in the grounds of Graceland and she would be employed as a secretary to the Elvis Presley fan club. She got into quite a lot of detail about what she would do when visitors came but then she stopped, saying, 'It's a waste of time, it won't come true'. It was suggested that it wouldn't come true if she didn't make a start: what was the first small step to making this dream come true? She said it was too big a dream, there was no point starting. So she was asked what skills she would need as secretary of the Elvis Presley fan club.

Elaine then discovered some of the skills she already possessed which could be used towards the dream; she had re-sat her English O level and gained a slightly better mark, she knew the music of Elvis Presley well, and she had studied his life in magazine articles. She decided that the first small step she needed to take was to find out about word processing courses so that she could handle the mail when she became secretary of a fan club (for more details see Milner 2001, pp.34–35).

TOP TIPS: FOR ADULTS 2
Bridge

Using a large sheet of paper, ask the person to draw a bridge with the problem at one end and the solution at the other. Then discuss how the person is going to make the journey, (i.e. in one fell swoop, with tiny steps), what obstacles they expect to encounter, who is needed to help them cross safely.

TOP TIPS: FOR ADULTS 3
From the past to the future
Life story work with people with dementia is crucial to goal setting with people who are not able to express their wishes. Time taken gathering information about a person's likes and dislikes and history generally will help goal planning.

Practice example: Goal setting

John is a resident in a home for elderly people. Staff report that he is disruptive in the dining room and keeps sliding down his chair. He pushes his food around and often needs feeding. He calls out constantly and is a nuisance to other residents in the dining room. He has lost some weight because sometimes he refuses to eat.

An interview with John's son provides the following information. Driving had been a large part of John's working life and the day he received a letter saying that his license was being taken away upset him deeply. He phoned his son, who went over and found him on the floor having suffered a stroke. John tried to go home after being in hospital, but this proved difficult with his mobility problems. He was using a Zimmer frame but had lots of small strokes.

His son says that John is very strong-willed and determined, a very loving and caring father who loved football. He isn't one for mixing socially, he doesn't like being in big crowds. He was not a big drinker but if he did go to the pub he would generally go with one person and sit in a corner. He enjoys the company of two to three people and he used to like listening to what was going on around him. He also likes listening to music.

He loves a cooked breakfast. He will eat it at any time of the day but needs help taking the rind taking off his bacon and cutting it up into small pieces. He doesn't like chicken at all, nor curries and stews, but likes very thinly sliced beef and ham. He loves corned beef sandwiches and would often have a slice of corned beef, mashed potato and fried egg. He has become very sweet toothed over the past few years and likes two to three sugars in his tea. He also likes to have ketchup on all his main meals. He would never eat pudding before.

(Baker 2015, p.68)

GOAL SETTING

Purpose: to carry out goal planning using life story material

1. List your concerns about, and goals for, John in the above example.

2. Utilising the information above, develop staff goals for helping John with his difficulties.

3. Prepare a care plan which addresses these.

(For two examples of a care plan using life story work, see Baker 2015, pp.68–72.)

Scaling progress and safety

Having asked the miracle question and explored the reply, de Shazer (1994) would follow up with a scaled question such as: suppose we had a scale from 0 to 10, and 0 was how things were when you first contacted us and 10 was the day after the miracle, how near to 10 are you today? These questions were developed by solution focused thinkers to help people express in a precise way what might otherwise be difficult to articulate. For example, suppose we had a scale from 0 to 100, where 0 is the pits and 100 is everything is fine, where are you on that scale today? The scale is set up in such a way that all the numbers are on the solution side (de Shazer 1994, p.104) but it is impossible to be sure what any number means, even for the person asked. They and we know that 50 is better than 40 and less good than 60, so answers provide a way of grading progress. But more importantly scaled questions and their answers help to make concrete what may be vague. The scale can vary as much as one wishes, for example 100 could represent the desired state at the end of the work with the person, or what that person would settle for, and so on. Similarly, scaled questions can be used in goal setting.

FOLLOW UP QUESTION PROMPTS TO ORIGINAL
SCALED QUESTIONS ABOUT THE PROBLEM/GOAL

- On a scale of 0 to 10, how satisfied are you with your score?

- When you are one point higher on the scale, what will *you* be doing differently?

- Where do you think [name of complainant] would put you on the scale?

- What will you be doing differently that will tell that person you are higher on the scale?

- On a scale of 0 to 10, suppose 0 was you couldn't be bothered and 10 was you would do absolutely anything to deal with the problem, where are you on that scale today?

- On a scale of 0 to 10, if 0 was very little confidence that you can succeed and 10 was fully confident, where are you today? (Follow up both these questions with what the person would be doing differently if one step higher.)

- If 10 is you know what you want and what you have to do, and 0 is the opposite, where are you on this scale?

The last three questions help the person decide whether they need to work on motivation, confidence or capacity in solving the problem. For example, a substance misuser is highly likely to know exactly what they need to do, not least because it is highly likely that they will have been preached at. It is more likely that they will need to work on increasing their determination to solve the problem or their confidence that they can do it. If a person gives a low score on either of these scales, the follow up question will be 'When you are one point higher, what will you be doing differently?' Shennan (2014) cautions against being tempted to argue a person higher up a low rating. If a person says they are at 0 or 1, then this is accepted and explored. For example, 'How come 1 and not 0? What's different to be at 1 and not 0?' Some people need a longer scale, especially teenagers and people who are seriously depressed. The former often like to have 1000 as their desired end point and the latter not infrequently go off the scale at the lower end. This doesn't matter as you can simply move into minus numbers.

Scaled questions are very useful in situations where there are safety issues. For example, in a child protection case you could ask: if 0 is the worst mother ever and 100 is a perfect mum, how would you rate your mothering? Very few people rate themselves at 100 so the answer will always provide you with space to talk about how they got to this point and how they can move further up the scale. And in child protection work, or for that matter any safety situations whether bullying or domestic violence, it is important to ask the person what score they think others would give them: 'You rate the safety of [name of vulnerable person/s] at 9; where do you think they would rate their safety?' Or 'Where do you think your social worker/ teacher, etc. would rate on you this scale?' And then, 'What do you need to do differently to convince that person that you are as safe as you say you are?'

Practice example:
Understanding safety

Alan has been disturbed several days before being detained under legal powers at his home. He resisted transfer by ambulance and was brought to the secure unit in handcuffs by the police. This is a section of his second interview on the unit.

Interviewer: So thinking about a scale of 0 to 10 where 10 is you out of hospital and things going well, and 0 is as bad as things were before, where are you right now on that scale?

Alan: Nought.

Interviewer: So how have you kept going when you are at nought?

Alan: Getting some sleep helped.

Interviewer: So sleep is really important for you. When you move up half a point on the scale what will be different for you?

Alan: I won't feel like hitting people.

Interviewer: Who did you feel like hitting?

Alan: The neighbours and that policeman. He had no right to put handcuffs on me.

Interviewer: How come the police were there?

Alan: I told the ambulance man I would cut him if he tried to come into my flat.

Interviewer: Have you cut anyone before? Or hit anyone?

Alan: No; but I would have done it.

Interviewer: How come you did not do that?

Alan: They came in before I could get a knife from the kitchen.

Interviewer: Do you still think about getting a knife for cutting someone?

Alan: I sometimes think about it.

Interviewer: How did you manage to think about it but not do it?

Alan: I think to myself that they will put me in hospital again if I cut someone. The neighbours might get me for it while I was sleeping.

Interviewer: Are there specific people that you think of cutting, neighbours or anyone else?

Alan: I felt like hitting that policeman.

Interviewer: Have you thought about cutting or hitting anyone in this hospital?

Alan: No.

Interviewer: How can we tell if you are thinking about cutting someone or hitting someone?

Alan: I don't know.

Interviewer: Will you tell us if you are thinking that?

Alan: [no reply]

Interviewer: When you're thinking like that, what can we do that will help?

Alan: Let me stay my room; the other people here are strange.

Interviewer: Will you tell us when you need to stay in your room?

Alan: Yes.

Interviewer: Okay; we will ask you if we are not sure. I guess that hitting or cutting someone would not help you get out of hospital sooner.

Alan: [nods]

Interviewer: Anything else to mention today?

Alan: No; I'm tired of talking just now.

(Macdonald 2011, p.164)

TOP TIPS: SCALED QUESTIONS FOR CHILDREN
1. Ladders
For children who are too young to understand numbers, draw steps or ladders to mark progress. Faces don't work so well as children tend not to like the sad or grumpy face at the one end of the scale.

2. Calendars
Rather than star charts, simply design a calendar and provide the child with stickers to place on each day when the behaviour agreed as a goal happens.

A SCALING WALK

Purpose: to bring scaling to life through experience
and highlight its main features

Ask everyone to think of a hobby or sport that they currently
engage in and at which they would like to be better. Set out
a scale of 1–10 along the room, with 1 = you are regularly
stuck at the worst you can imagine it can be for you and
10 is you performing consistently at your personal peak.
Place yourself on the scale. Discuss with the person nearest
to you:

- How did you get to this point?

- What does 10 represent?

- Where would you like to be?

- What do you need to do to get to this point?

- What help might you require?

- Who would be best placed to help you?

MORE SCALING

Purpose: to provide a practice opportunity in asking scaled questions

- Consider the last piece of work you undertook with a service user.

- On a scale of 0–10, where 0 is the worst work you could have done, and 10 is the very best, where would you rate this piece of work?

- What would you have been doing differently if you had been able to rate it at the next highest number?

- How would the service user have known that you were doing it at the higher number?

- How would your supervisor have known that you were doing it at the higher number?

- What will you be doing differently to achieve the higher number next time?

YET MORE SCALING

Purpose: to provide a practice opportunity in asking scaled questions

- Make a list of the things that a professional people-worker does that tell you they are good at their job.

- Scale yourself about whether you do these things Not at all; Sometimes; Most of the Time or Always.

- Think about the things that you do Sometimes.

- When do you do these?

- What is happening when you are doing them?

- When was the last time you did them?

- How can you do more of them so that tomorrow you are doing them Most of the Time?

SCALING A PROJECT

Purpose: to practise asking scaled questions; experience scaling firsthand; and practise asking for the details of solutions

Choose a project you are currently engaged on but are not making as much progress with as you would like. This could be stopping smoking, losing weight, landscaping a garden, doing home improvements or passing a course of study, for example. It is important to choose an emotionally charged project. In pairs, create a scale for your project and interview each other to find out:

- Where you are on the scale?

- What you did to get there?

- Where you want to be and in what time frame?

- Do you want to progress in small or large steps?

- What is the smallest step you could take right now towards your goal?

- What are your chances of doing this?

- What will people notice differently about you when you have taken this small step?

- What difference will it make to you?

Practice example:
Using scaling to create solutions ▪▪▪▪▪▪▪▪▪▪▪

Nurse: Hello Sam, remember me, I'm Jane. Thanks for talking yesterday about the surgery that is planned. We talked a lot. You showed that you have a good understanding of the actual procedure as well as the risks associated with it. We also talked about the anxious feelings you have. As we agreed yesterday, today we will be spending some time getting to know your situation more deeply, what your concerns are, as well as your goals in working together with me. How does that sound?

Sam: That sounds okay. What would you like to know?

Jane: Well, there's a lot I don't know, and I'm not an expert on you, you are. But I guess a good place to begin with would be with our situation, our relationship right now. Sam, I wonder if you could tell me, what needs to come out of this meeting so that you can say this is helpful?

Sam: I don't know. Maybe to feel less anxious, to feel like I can take charge of these jangly nerves, I don't know, to feel more confident that I think I can get through this.

Jane: Okay, so it sounds like what you want is to feel more in control of the Jangly Nerves. Let's look at these Jangly Nerves in closer detail. On a scale of 1–10 (1 being least, 10 being worst) how would you rate those Jangly Nerves now?

Sam: I'd say 6.

Jane: And where on the scale you like to be, so that you have felt calm and okay.

Sam: I'd say a 4 would look good.

Jane: All right 4 would be good. And how would 5 feel?

Sam: If I could get to feeling 5 by the end of today, then that would be a great start.

Jane: Yes, I agree, it really would. So let's talk about those Jangly Nerves some more. Sam, when do they seem more obvious, more out there?

Sam: I have no idea. They're always there.

Jane: Well, suppose I asked your wife to answer that question. What you think she'd say?

Sam: That's easy, she'd say it's whenever something happens that might take me away from always being in charge. She says I just hate it when things happen that I can't control.

Jane: Oh, that's interesting. So now, I wonder what your wife would say you are like when you are calm. Do you think she'd be able to think of times when your Jangly Nerves are not so apparent?

Sam: She'd probably say I'm calm when I've had a holiday, when I'm lying in my hammock reading a detective story. As a matter of fact those are some times when I'm quite okay.

Jane: So, suppose a miracle happened overnight, and the Jangly Nerves just went away. What would you be doing and feeling, can you describe that to me?

Sam: I'd be cool, calm, collected, able to go into that surgery knowing that I was doing the right thing, and pretty much accepting of the surgeon's skills.

Jane: Maybe if we tried using some of the cool, calmness that seems to come out when you are lying in that hammock, and applying it to this situation, your Jangly Nerves might be less obvious. What you think?

Sam: Well, I'm willing to give it a try...

(McAlistair 2007, pp.41–142)

ASSESSING CONFIDENCE

Purpose: to experience scaled questions

- On a Confidence scale of 0–10, where 0 is not at all and 10 is completely, how confident are you about using solution focused approaches?

- If you were to rate yourself at the next highest number, what would you be doing differently?

- How would you have achieved this?

- What do you have to do to make this happen?

- What qualities do you have that will help to make this happen?

PERSONALISING SCALED QUESTIONS

**Purpose: to practise developing
creative questions**

Thinking of a person with whom you are currently working, devise a set of scaled questions that are unique to that person.

Evaluating the session

Where the decision is for the person to simply do more of what is working, there is frequently no need for a second session. However people often wish to report on their successes, and sometimes successes need strengthening through telling. Sometimes minor adjustments are necessary but, as a general rule, you don't need to commit yourself or the people you are working with to a set number of sessions. Quite simply the work takes as long as it takes, although it is often brief. People can be surprised that they have solved their problems quickly but the necessity for further sessions is clarified by asking them how they will know their problems have been solved, what they will be doing differently and what other people will notice.

You also do not need to see people every week as this can be burdensome for them. They may wish to space their discussion of painful issues more widely or their progress may well be uneven. It is discouraging not to have any progress to report. Where a second session is obviously indicated, we consult with the person over how long they think it will take to do the tasks they have decided upon and set the next date accordingly. Sessions do not necessarily need to be one hour long; they can be much shorter. It is worth adding that an appointment can be brought forward or put back as necessary. Careful spacing of sessions appears to reduce the number of overall number of sessions required. For example one woman who had multiple problems and set herself multiple goals thought it would take a month to begin her 'miracle day'. She rang to put her appointment back another month and then arrived having successfully completed all her goals. The session was used to allow her to talk about how she did it and highlight the personal qualities her substantial success revealed.

Also important at this stage of the first session is evaluating how useful the session has been, whether it was what the person expected and what would have been more useful. People are invariably polite when asked these questions so we build checks against any complacency on our part. For example when a person says it was a bit helpful, we add, 'Oh dear, that's not good enough. What would I have been doing differently if I had been more helpful?' We also make it plain that our notes are open for revision and that the person can add any ideas, clarify our thinking about their problem and solutions and correct inaccuracies. This is followed up in the covering letter accompanying the session notes. We find that young people are the most likely to request amendments, usually simple matters of detail, and sometimes people whose cultural realities are different and we haven't completely understood them. For example Indira requested numerous detailed changes to the notes outlining her tangled dowry arrangements but no changes to the comments about her emotional response to these. We always make these corrections in view of the person at subsequent sessions and send out amended notes. In this way we hope to be no more than an influential part in the co-authoring of new life stories, not experts in other people's lives.

Evaluation questions

- How is this conversation going for you?

- Should we keep talking about this or would you be more interested in...?

- Is this interesting to you? Is this what we should spend time talking about?

- I was wondering if you would be more interested in me asking some more about this or whether we should focus on...?

- What would we be talking about if I was being more helpful?

- What question haven't I asked that you wish I had?

- On a scale of 1–10 where 1 is this session has not been at all helpful and 10 is it couldn't have been better, where would rate this session?

- If you had scored the session one point higher, what would I have been doing differently?

- If you had scored this session one point higher, what would you have doing differently?

Suggested end of session tasks when progress is slow

- Each day do one small thing that is good for you. We'll talk about what difference it makes.

- Each day notice what else you do that is good for you, so we can talk about it.

- Keep track of the good choices you make so we can talk about them.

- As you are not yet able to *defeat* the problem, what can you do to stop it growing, or to make it wait (so you will be taking a little control back for yourself)? Start with small steps.

- Pretend you have a future and notice the difference, so we can talk about it. Notice what you will be doing instead of what you do now.

- Do something to be kind to yourself and hard on the problem, then notice what you will be doing, or feeling differently.

- Problems try to control us, so confuse the problem by taking some control of your own thoughts. Think up some things to say to yourself that will help you to stand up to the problem and its lies. I'll be interested in what you come up with.

Where subsequent sessions are indicated, they follow exactly the same format as the first session, other than beginning by asking 'What is better?' How the person achieved improvement is explored, goals are revisited where necessary, and the person is asked if these changes are good enough.

3

Specific Contexts

It will be clear by now that solution focused questions can be developed for use in any situation but workers new to solution focused practice tell us that they worry about not having enough relevant questions. These will develop as they become confident in listening to what the person says before framing their next question to fit what has just been said but, as a starter, we outline some questions for specific situations which have not been covered in the text so far, or may not have been covered in sufficient detail.

Terminally ill people

The main issues here are many workers' reluctance to talk about death and how to balance encouragement to be hopeful whilst still recognising and validating the fear, and possibly pain, that accompany terminal illness. Walsh (2010, p.173) discusses the ethical frameworks which guide work in these situations, briefly: do some good; avoid harm; respect autonomy; and be fair. Additionally she adds confidentiality, truth telling and informed consent. Being truthful doesn't mean the need to be brutally blunt; rather it means the need to explore the goals a person has for the life they have still to live. Where a child is receiving palliative care for a terminal illness, the quality of the remaining time is vital, so establishing the child's goals is a matter of urgency. Gardiner (1977) outlines the rights of a dying child:

- to know the truth about the probable outcome of their illness or, as most children have already worked it out for themselves, to affirm the truth

- to share thoughts about dying – not just the probability of death but the many questions that follow

- to live as full and normal a life as possible

- to participate in the process of dying. To have a say whether treatment continues or not, and whether to die in hospital, at home or in a hospice.

Questions for goal setting with terminally ill people

- What will be different when you have control over your pain?

- What will be good enough pain control for you?

- What ideas do you have about what comes after this life?

- How will things look better for you when you have worked out what it will look like?

- How do you want your life to be between now and [next week, next month, etc.]?

- What are your best achievements?

- What hopes do you still have?

- What do you best want to be remembered for?

- What small changes in living differently will make dying a 'good death'?

- Imagine the day after you die – you're looking back and discovering that you're pleased with all the things that happened between now and then. What will be telling you that it went well, that you did yourself justice?

- When you're on your deathbed, what will you not be regretting?

- In here (hospice/hospital) how have you managed to keep going? What have you kept doing that you would normally be doing outside? Have you surprised yourself with how you've dealt with it? How will you know when you're dealing with it even better?

The question about what will not be regretted – what has life been for you? – is important for people who want to talk about injustices in their lives which have never before been aired. Wright (2003) found that being in hospice care and separated from their partners provided opportunities for many older women to talk about a life of domestic violence. Knowing that the abuse would end due to their imminent death enabled them to break the silence about their experiences and gain comfort from this.

DILEMMAS

Purpose: to consider solutions to dilemmas

Mary is an 82-year-old patient in a nursing home. She has vascular dementia and her condition has deteriorated in recent months. She is now in end-stage dementia. Mary is refusing to eat. Medical staff need to make a decision on whether to commence artificial peg feeding, a procedure that causes discomfort and a certain amount of pain as well as the risk of infection and complications. Her family is distressed and adamant that she must not be starved.

How can this ethical dilemma be solved?

(For more details see Walsh 2010, p.177)

Suicide

Hawkes *et al.* (1998, p.103) maintain that suicidal people have a specific deficit in problem-solving skills. It is this difficulty in generating alternative solutions to problems that the miracle question, exception questions and scaling questions help to redress. If you take suicide as one attempted solution to a problem – but only one of many – you reduce blame for the person and value the difficult nature of their situation. You invite them to wonder if this is the only valid solution. Thus an initial answer to the miracle question may be, 'I'd be dead'. This answer indicates the seriousness of the situation but then you would ask 'How would that help?', beginning to separate suicide from what the person wants to be different, which may have nothing to do with death. Exception questions and scaling questions introduce the idea of movement and possibility.

Questions for people who are feeling suicidal

- This option seems very hard on you, how do you deserve that?

- Did the overdose help?

- What could you do instead that will be easier on you?

- You must have a good reason for hurting yourself…?

- Supposing in six months or so, you have to look back and see this meeting as something that turned out to be the best, how would you know?

- If 0 is not at all and 100 is completely, how interested in the future are you?

John Henden (2008) has developed these questions further:

- Tell me about a time in the last week when you felt least suicidal.

- Before you were feeling as you do at the moment, what did you do in the day that interested you?

- What has stopped you taking your life up to this point?

- On a scale of 1–10, how suicidal do you feel right now? How suicidal were you before you decided to seek help? What would be you be doing/thinking/feeling that would be half a point higher?

- What have you done in the last couple of weeks that has made a difference to this terrible situation you are in?

- On a scale of 1–10, how determined are you to give other options (other than suicide) a try first?

- What would happen in this session for you to think it was worthwhile coming?

- Let's suppose you went for the last resort option and actually died. You are at your own funeral as a spirit, looking down from about ten feet at the mourners below. What might you be thinking about another option you could have tried first? Which of the mourners would be most upset? What advice would they have wanted to give you about other options?

- When was the last time before this current time that you thought of ending it all? What did you do then that made a difference and enabled you to pull yourself back?

- Let us suppose for one minute that you decide not to go for this option and you live to a ripe old age. You are looking back on your life as a person who survived this dark period and lived a purposeful and meaningful life. What would your life have been like? What sorts of things would you have done? What new people would you have known? What sort of places might you have visited? What sort of holidays would you have had? What other challenges in life might you have had to resolve? How would you have allocated time in your retirement? Where might you have seen the best sunrises and sunsets?

- Suppose you decided not to go ahead with this last resort option and you are much older and wiser than you are now. What advice would you give to you now to solve this problem/get through this time of difficulty?

HOPE FROM DESPAIR

Purpose: to begin to think about ways out of despair and into hope

- Identify one client or service user who appears despairing and hopeless.

- What, if anything, do you know about what really matters in their life?

- Construct some solution focused questions that would allow you to open up options for this person.

(Adapted from Walsh 2010, p.144)

People with chronic illness or disability

Although developed as a solution focused tool to help children manage illness better, a pictorial cube is helpful in work with adults too (see images on next page). Using the metaphor of a turtle (slow, but long lived) captaining a ship, the person is invited to consider that although they may be disabled they are still captain of their own ship and need the crew (the professionals) to do what the captain needs them to do. The cube can be rolled as a dice to determine how the conversation will start, or can be used for group activity.[1]

---

1   For more information, contact Gerd Nysethen@helse nordtrondelag.no

Illustrations by Knut Hoihjelle knut.hoihjelle@namdalsavisa.no

People who hear voices

We have discussed earlier how to explore goals with people who are mentally ill. Here we describe questions that can be used with people who hear voices.

Questions for people who find their voices distressing

- What are the voices saying to you?

- Are these voices for you or against you?

- These voices throw you into confusion, whose interests are served by this?

- Are there times when you have been able to stand up to the voices?

- How did you do this?

- What is it like for the voices to have to listen to your thoughts for a while?

- What it is like for them when they know you are developing mistrust of them?

- How do you cope when the voices are bothering you a lot?

- What do people notice differently about you when you are standing up to the voices?

Practice example:
Exploring voices

Ruth: I'm doing alright in my course but I'm taking these drugs. It says on the bottle that they're for acute and chronic schizophrenia. They get rid of the voices but they make me feel hung over 14 hours a day. The doctor says just take them at night but this doesn't help. Don't make me sleep any better and I feel dreadful all the time. When I complain, he says, 'So what's worse? Feeling groggy or having voices? Don't complain'. Once they've written the prescription, that's it. End of interest. I'm still getting the voices on and off.

Counsellor: What are they saying to you?

Ruth: The same old stuff. Nothing new.

Counsellor: Dad's old criticisms?

Ruth: It's like a bloke's voice… Not someone I recognised. Not dad's. It's very critical. Reinforces your insecurities.

Counsellor: What do you say back?

Ruth: My voice is sarcastic.

Counsellor: What you think the purpose of this voice is, what does it want?

Ruth: When you start to achieve something, it's a constant reminder not to let you do it. I get ready to go out. I'm up for this. And then the voices kick in and you don't go. And then feel worse for not going. When you decide not to go, you don't have to face it but…it's won. Stopped you doing it. Feel crap because people ask you out, you don't go and then they stop asking you. Think you're a mood swinging person. It is difficult to explain 10 minutes before going out. One housemate knows. She does excuses for me.

Counsellor: Could you do anything else to help?

Ruth: She says, 'tell them to fuck off'. She doesn't agree with me taking the prescription. I take it for a few days and then cope for a few days.

Counsellor: How do you do coping on these days?

Ruth: Denial. It's like someone is talking in the background and it's there but I'm not listening... And that's really hard to do when there's important things to do. Can't say, I'm not [going] to write this essay.

Counsellor: What effect does it have on the voices when you stand up to them?

Ruth: It doesn't affect them. It has an effect on how I feel... more positive. When I feel more positive, I can go out. It doesn't make them go away.

(Milner and O'Byrne 2002, pp.146–147)

People who are disabled with stress

Stress is a normal part of life. Having problems is normal. Life is full of problems. Once you solve one problem another comes along. However an accumulation of stresses can overstretch a person's normal coping capacity and, like people who are suicidal or depressed, multiple stress makes for difficulty in generating alternative solutions to their problems. Looking in the misery cupboard will only yield more miseries but the miracle question can open up possibilities and help the person refocus on what they want out of life as is illustrated below.

Practice example:
Using the miracle question

Counsellor: When you wake up in the morning what would be the first sign the miracle has happened?

Client: I don't know.

Counsellor: So what would you be seeing when...?

Client: I would feel as if I had got my life back.

Counsellor: How would you know? What would be the first sign for you that you started to get your life back?

Client: My partner and I will be sleeping in the same bed for a start.

Counsellor: That has not been happening for a while?

Client: We had decided a while ago that I should sleep in the spare bed because I was always coming to bed late and waking her up. I was waking up during the night as well, because I was tossing and turning in my sleep. I would wake up early and not be able to get back to sleep and then I would wake her up again. We were both exhausted and bad tempered in the morning so we decided that for a while I would sleep next door.

Counsellor: So after the miracle, what would be happening?

Client: I would be getting a decent night's sleep and we would be back together in bed.

Counsellor: What would be the first thing that would need to happen to give you a chance at a better night's sleep?

Client: I thought about not working at home so much at night. When I go to bed my head's still full of problems and worries.

Counsellor: So after the miracle you will be working less in the evening – not right until you go to bed – and you would have found ways of drawing a line under the day. What sort of things would you have done?

Client: I would spend some time with my partner before she goes to bed, maybe just watch television together. I think I am withdrawing from everyone because I feel so stressed. My partner is fed up with it and we have had rows about it.

Counsellor: So after the miracle you would finish work earlier and spend more time with your partner in the evening. What else?

(O'Connell 2001, pp.71–72)

4

Surviving Trauma and Violence

People who have been traumatised by events, whether they are physical or sexual assaults or the unexpected loss of a very close relationship, often internalise their problems. They may be devastated by the destruction of relationships; suffer low self-esteem; have a stronger sense of lack of control over their lives; tend to self-blame; and take responsibility for problems beyond what is reasonable and realistic.

They may be so overwhelmed with how things are right now that they find it difficult to think what life could be like. In these instances, a search for exceptions without some attention paid to distress, pain and failure would neglect to identify what is productive blame and other-directed anger – both behaviours that can be used to help a person begin to think about how life can be better. This chapter looks at how these can be addressed by paying attention to personal issues and their meanings to people, using tentative language. Tentative language prefaces statements with 'perhaps', 'could it be' and 'I wonder'.

Practice example:
The realities of violence

Jackie (15 years old) is talking about her father's drinking. 'One night he came back from the pub, he smashed my face against the wall. There was blood all down the wall. I was whimpering on the floor like a puppy and he said, "Look at that mess you've made on the wall. Clean it up." The next day my face was all swollen and he put his hand on my face and he said, "My poor baby, what have you done? How did you get like that?" He took me to the hospital and he was being so nice. You see, he gets drunk and then he can't remember. What I want to know is, why? Not why me. I'm glad I got it and not my mum. Why did he do it? If he tells me why, I'd know it wasn't my fault. Maybe it is my fault? I've been giving myself some reasons.'

The techniques described in Chapter 2 work effectively with traumatised people. However where people feel particularly vulnerable in decision-making, it can be helpful to suggest ways in which they can be kind to themselves, comfort themselves and find ways of feeling safer. In this chapter, we outline techniques for these special situations, but first we revisit the questions which acknowledge not only how difficult the person's situation is but also recognise accomplishments which may seem modest – and thus are often discounted – unless the adverse circumstances in which they have occurred are highlighted:

Survival questions

- Given all the difficulties you have had, how have you managed to survive?

- Can you tell me about the times you can cope despite this feeling?

- How did you do it?

- What have you learned about yourself during these difficulties?

- Can we use any of this in your current difficulties?

- In times of difficulty, who or what has been helpful?

- Who could help you?

- How do you find this person?

- What do you think it is about you that got them to respond to you?

- Do you think you can rely on them helping your current difficulty?

Practice example: Domestic violence

Thelma has recently left her husband after years of physical and emotional abuse but is facing a number of legal battles over her divorce, contact with her daughter and compensation for her husband selling her house and furniture behind her back. She is also struggling with the fact that he is pleading with her to take him back (she still has some feelings for him) and the financial pressures of living in a rented house she can't afford. She says that she can see no future for herself now that she is getting older, and feels like giving up.

When asked how she keeps going even though she feels like giving up (a lot more than one question is asked), Thelma says she still takes care of her appearance, walks the dog each day and helps relatives. Although she can see no joy at the moment, she can remember times when she was joyful. She keeps going because she has hope and reminds herself of this by having red roses in the house.

Survival of poor parenting scale

Not everyone is blessed with a happy home life, although we are all expected to love our parents – who may well have done little to earn any love at all. Because of societal ideas about happy families, we find that people who have ended up in care, or generally been scapegoated in their family or neglected, have a tendency to think they must be to blame in some way. To help them decide on goals for a happier life, we often ask them to fill in the following scale which is adapted from Yvonne Dolan's work with sexually abused women (Dolan 1991). Each item is chosen to reflect the essential components of resilience: disclosures being positively received, thinking positively, having supportive friends, achievement and success. The scale can also be adapted for use in a variety of situations, such as recovery from sexual abuse, substance abuse, bullying, and so on.

★

SURVIVAL OF POOR PARENTING SCALE

No.	Tick the box that fits best	Not at all	Just a little	Pretty much	Very much
1	Able to talk about what happened				
2	Able to talk about other things				
3	Able to grieve about what happened				
4	Able to cope with guilt about what happened				
5	Able to express anger about what happened				
6	Feels part of a new family				
7	Stands up for self				
8	Sleeps well				
9	Eats well				
10	Keeps smart				
11	Goes to social events				
12	Copes with new situations				
13	Meets new friends				
14	Laughs				
15	Able to choose supportive relationships				
16	Able to relax				
17	Able to tolerate criticism				
18	Able to accept praise				
19	Interested in the future				
20	Likes self				
21	Goes to school/work				
22					
23					
24					

Safety and control

When an experience of violence shatters a person's illusion of safety, s/he often loses further control over his/her life, for example, not venturing out without an escort, wearing 'big clothes' or experiencing panic attacks or flashbacks. The reality of life for many people is that it is not very safe. The person may have been abused by one person but there is always the potential for abuse by many others so it is never a simple case of helping people come to terms with just one bad experience; they need to develop a range of effective safety strategies. For example, when Danny gave up dealing cocaine, he still took down previous customers' telephone numbers when approached for drugs so that it wasn't known he was no longer dealing. Had this become widely known his safety would have been compromised. Similarly he continued to give people what he referred to as 'the eye', that is a hard stare. In our work with a group of teenage girls who were at risk of being drawn into substance misuse and prostitution by older men, they were assisted in developing a safety plan which enabled them to go out together safely on Saturday evenings. They ensured their mobile phones were fully charged, that they had each other's numbers, they pre-booked a taxi for going home, went to the toilet in pairs, and one of them agreed to stay sober so that she could look out for the rest. A person at risk of domestic violence may be encouraged to construct a 'get out quick' kit, comprised of items such as a spare key (to avoid being locked in), a supply of cash, a spare mobile phone, a toothbrush and a spare pair of pants. Items of the kit are commonly hidden in places the assailant is unlikely to look, such as cake-making ingredients in kitchen cupboards.

A not uncommon response to feeling a complete lack of control is for people to give up any hope of safety and become reckless. Here we use 'peace of mind' questions. These are questions for use where you are concerned about the safety of a person's situation. This could be a grown-up living with domestic violence, a young man in a gang or young women at risk from getting drunk at the weekend. When asked in a spirit of 'for my peace of mind', nagging and lecturing are avoided.

- How do I know that you will be all right?

- What can you do, and what can I do, to help me understand that you will be all right?

- What are the things that make me know you are going to be all right?

- Could you tell me about them? I might feel a whole lot better about it all if I knew those things.

Bedtime therapy

People report that flashbacks, intrusive thoughts and feelings of worthlessness are most likely to occur in the period between going to bed and falling asleep, with sleep not infrequently being interrupted by nightmares. To help people in this situation we have devised what we call 'bedtime therapy' and it can also be used to help people who find sleep difficult where the bedroom is actually associated with the abuse. People are encouraged to plan how to make their bath and bedroom routine warmer and safer. This can be quite simple; for example, David simply needed to sleep on the other side of his bed, away from the door. Other people change the entire decor or even move the furniture about and add some comfort symbols to remind them of enjoyable times. Changes to bathroom routines can be more complex; for example, Shona had difficulty in looking at her body and showered with the light off because she saw her body as dirty and defiled. After much discussion she opted for a bathtime routine which consisted of a cool shower with unperfumed soap (medicated soap had connotations with the original abuse) to wash off the 'dirt' and imagine it going down the plug hole. She would then have a warm shower with her favourite perfumed soap and dry herself with a fluffy towel. Where people are troubled by nightmares, we have found that they can actually change the ending by getting out of bed, taking a short break and thinking of a new ending. For example, Shenaz would go to the toilet and imagine she was urinating on the abuser as he appeared in her nightmare.

SOLUTIONS FOR YOU

Purpose: to consider how solution focused questioning can be used in a reflective way

Rate yourself on the following scales:

- If 0 is not at all and 10 is completely satisfied, how do you feel about how you look?

- If 0 is not at all and 10 is all the time, how much time do you spend thinking about, or discussing with friends and colleagues, how best you can manage your health?

- If 0 is never and 10 is every other month, how often have you started either a new diet or an exercise regime?

- Is there a different way in which you could look at your body?

6, 5, 4, 3, 2, 1

Intrusive thoughts can make getting off to sleep very difficult. Here a routine adapted from Dolan (1998) works very well, partly because the slow, shallow breathing reduces panicky feelings (for more details, see Macdonald, 2011, Appendix 11), and partly because it is so very boring and repetitive. We ask the person to make their self as comfortable as possible in bed and then start to say to themselves six things they can actually feel. For example, 'I can feel the fresh sheet on my chin, I can feel my hands touching lightly on my chest, I can feel my toes touching the bed clothes' and so on. Then we ask them to say six things that they can hear, for example, 'I can hear the clock ticking, I can hear the heating system clicking, I can hear the radiator creaking'. We then move on to six things they can see. Obviously, because their eyes are closed, they have to say six times that they can see darkness. This darkness can be discussed to discover what a helpful darkness would be like: for example, 'I can see a black velvet curtain and I'm sinking into it'. They are asked to accompany this exercise with slow, shallow breathing so that they take in one breath for each element of the exercise; and, if an intrusive thought intervenes, they start at the top again – however many times it occurs. This exercise demands a fair amount of determination but it does work.

TOP TIPS: INVISIBLE CROCODILES FOR CHILDREN

Where a small child is troubled with intrusive thoughts and flashbacks, we offer to lend the child one of our invisible crocodiles. We explain that these crocodiles live under the bed and eat bad thoughts, all nasty things, and that they especially like a nightmare as a special treat, which is like ice cream with chocolate sauce to them. We ask them what colour crocodile they would like and build up a vivid picture of this crocodile living under their bed, eating all their troubling thoughts (they frequently choose a crocodile with gold wings). We ask the adult in their life to be careful not to knock the crocodile when they clean the bedroom as the crocodile sleeps quietly during the day. We then say that we have exactly such a crocodile in stock and as it has got rather thin through lack of food, we will send it this very night. When the crocodile has done its job, we ask if we can take it back for another child.

Being sensibly selfish

Like Jackie at the beginning of this section, many people who have had abusive experiences take quite unreasonable and unachievable responsibility for events. This can be challenged by asking curious questions about what reasonable responsibility-taking would look like; for example, how can a person be sensibly selfish?

CURIOUS QUESTIONING

Purpose: to practise devising curious questions

- Re-read the practice example of Jackie at the beginning of this section.

- Devise at least three curious questions that would challenge Jackie's ideas about self-blame.

Doormat therapy

When a person is spinning plates to keep a difficult family or work situation going, we ask that person who comes first in their family or group, ranking every member. In families, most people place the children first, the partner second, then other relatives and finally the family pet. People often forget to rank themselves in the family and need to be reminded that they have just told you that they are at the bottom of the pile – on the doormat. Curious questions about how someone occupying such a lowly position in the family or workplace can possibly be responsible for everyone else's actions, thoughts and feelings are useful here. Follow-up questions would include:

- If you think it would be selfish to put yourself first, how could you make a start on putting yourself a strong second? Or third?

- What things are other people good at but don't get the chance to do as you are taking all the responsibility?

- What sort of responsibility-taking do you think other people would like to develop?

- Who in your family/group could help more?

Practice example:
Rising above the doormat

Janice, hopeless and depressed with no sense of control in her life, was caring for her own three children, a recently deceased brother's two teenagers, and, at weekends, her partner's two toddlers from a previous relationship as well as holding down a part-time job. On top of all this responsibility, she was also being assessed by Social Care following her application to be made official foster parent to her brother's children. The scrutiny of Social Care was an extra burden, especially as they were recommending that she give up her part-time job to concentrate on the children. This would not only reduce her income but also remove the one situation where she could forget her worries and be reminded of her strengths.

Janice picked up the doormat metaphor, commenting that everyone wipes their feet on her. To get herself up a tiny bit from the bottom, she thought that the children could help more and this led to identifying their abilities and strengths. The eldest was good with the other children; the next one was good at washing up; the youngest girl was good at making people laugh; and so on. Janice's suggested homework task was to utilise all these competences to lessen the burden on her, and she reported triumphantly at the next session that she was no longer a doormat: 'I'm at kitchen sink level now!'

Comfort cues

Dolan (1998) suggests learning how to comfort oneself also makes it more likely that people will begin to value themselves. Being able to self-comfort also lessens the impact of a traumatic experience or a flashback or panic attack. Of Dolan's many exercises and ideas, we have found developing a 'comfort cue' and creating a 'comfort drawer' to be particularly helpful. Creating a comfort drawer is a simple and pleasant task; it consists of filling a drawer – or box – with things which remind the person of their successes, support systems and hopes. So, for example, a comfort drawer might contain a certificate or a baby scan to symbolise success; a photograph of friends or a list of telephone numbers to indicate where support can be found; perhaps a key ring to remind a person of a hope to learn to drive or, as in Thelma's case, a vase of roses to remind her of hope. A favourite CD or bar of chocolate can also be included for a shot of instant comfort. The comfort drawer is there as a resource at times of stress.

COMFORT CUES

Purpose: to practise developing a comfort cue

Think of a time when life was good. Select a snapshot of this time and visualise what was happening:

- What could you see?

- What could you hear?

- What could you smell?

- What could you feel – physically, not emotionally?

- What one sensation brings back this scene most vividly?

- If you could distil this one sensation, what would it be?

- Or could one thing symbolise this sensation?

This is your comfort cue.

Treats

Finding solutions to problems is hard work so we often ask people to do something which is good for them or have a treat that evening as a way of rewarding their effort. We found out from evaluation questions that 'doing the treat thing' is also very helpful for people who are experiencing low self-worth. Asked what had been most helpful, Sally replied, 'The treats... I didn't take it that seriously at first; I thought you were just being nice. But it built up. It made me realise I am worth a treat. I felt really good doing the treats.' And encouraging people to be good to themselves is not just for women; we find that the toughest of men also enjoy the luxury of a treat or a spot of bathtime therapy.

Living well is the best revenge

Dolan (1998) makes a distinction between surviving abuse, which limits a person almost as much as remaining a victim, and living a life of joy. To live a life of joy and fulfilment, old hurts and resentments need to go. She has many suggestions for dealing with anger and upset, including 'Write, Read, Burn' and 'A Letter to the Abuser'.

In the former, the person is asked to write down every detail of the hurt – a task that may take several days (we worked with one person who wrote seventy pages detailing their anger). It is then read and burnt, although we offer people the choice of how to dispose of the writing. Some choose to travel to the seaside where they tear up the writing and then throw it into the sea. Some like to dispose of it in a rubbish bin. And occasionally people decide to wrap it up in a shoe box, seal the lid and store it in the loft – just in case they may want to revisit it at some later date, not that we know of anyone who has done so.

'A Letter to the Abuser' is a rather more complicated procedure. Again the person is asked to write down everything they want the person who has harmed them to hear, and to take their time over this. When they are satisfied that they have written enough, they are asked to write two letters to themselves. The first is the letter they think the abuser would send in reply, knowing full well that they are going to get a whole load of excuses. Then they write the letter of apology they would like to receive. This process works well for many people as it separates and highlights two realities: the fact that the abuser is a miserable person who is unable to face up to what they have done and is thus despicable (and not worth losing sleep over), and the fact that the person who was harmed is of value and worth an apology.

Although most of these exercises were designed to help women who had experienced sexual abuse, they can be adapted to a whole range of situations where anger and resentments are preventing a person from living a good life, such as warring couples. On a simpler level, you can ask the person not to put another bean in the 'resentment jar' until they have taken one out and thrown it away.

TOP TIPS: IDEAS FOR WORKING WITH CHILDREN

Helping hands

Ask the child to draw an outline of their hand and write the name of someone who they trust to help them on each digit, and how they will contact them (add telephone numbers if the child is not in regular contact with this person). Some children have an impoverished helping circle but may well have a trusted pet or toy. Talking to a pet or toy is a whole lot less threatening than talking to a professional worker.

Secret signs

Where a child is living with a family where there have been child protection concerns, agree a secret sign that would alert a trusted adult that the child wanted help. This could be moving a certain ornament or providing the child with a blank stamped addressed postcard.

Secret thoughts box

Decorate a shoe box and make a letterbox slit in the top. Invite the child to write down any worries and post them in the box. Invite the adults to write down any good things they have noticed about the child and post these. After tea on Friday and before the weekend starts, an adult opens the box and reads out the worries and compliments. As a worry is read out, ask the child if it is still a worry – not infrequently the worry has gone with the posting. If the worry is still there, this can be addressed at a time when the adult is able to concentrate fully on the child's concerns.

Internet Resources

www.brief-therapy.org for the USA Centre, for books and videos etc. It also has handouts and essays to download. There is an international discussion/helpline (called a LIST) which professionals can join through this site: click on relevant links, then on Harry and Jocelyn Korman, then on subscribe SFT-L and follow the instructions.

www.brieftherapy.org.uk for the London Brief Therapy Centre.

www.btne.org for Brief Therapy North-East (Newcastle).

www.talkingcure.com for research results worldwide, mainly USA.

References

Baker, C. (2015) *Developing Excellent Care for People Living with Dementia in Care Homes.* London: Jessica Kingsley Publishers.

Berg, I. K. and Miller, S. D. (1992) *Working with the Problem Drinker: A Solution Focused Approach.* New York: W. W. Norton & Co.

Berg, I.K. and Reuss, H.H. (1998) *Solutions Step by Step: A Substance Abuse Treatment Manual.* London: W.W. Norton & Co.

Berg, I.K. and Steiner, T. (2003) *Children's Solution Work.* London: W.W.Norton.

Couzens, A. (1999) 'Sharing the Load: Group Conversations with Young Indigenous Men.' In *Extending Narrative Therapy: A Collection of Practice-Based Papers.* Adelaide: Dulwich Centre Publications.

de Shazer, S. (1988*)* Clues: Investigating Solutions in Brief Therapy.* New York: W.W. Norton & Co.

de Shazer, S. (1991) *Putting Difference to Work.* London: W.W. Norton & Co.

de Shazer, S. (1994) *Words Were Originally Magic.* New York: W.W. Norton & Co.

Dolan, Y. (1991) *Resolving Child Abuse.* New York: W.W. Norton & Co.

Dolan, Y. (1998) *One Small Step: Moving Beyond Trauma to a Life of Joy.* Watsonville, CA: Papier-Mache Press.

Fiske, H. and Zalter, B. (2005) 'Solution Focused Scavenger Hunt.' In T.S. Nelson (ed.) *Education and Training in Solution Focused Brief Therapy.* Binghampton, NY: The Howarth Press.

Gardiner, G. (1977) 'The rights of dying children: Some personal reflections.' *Psychotherapy Bulletin 10,* 20–23.

Ghul, R. (2005) 'Moan, Moan, Moan.' In T.S. Nelson (ed.) *Education and Training in Solution Focused Brief Therapy.* Binghampton, NY: The Howarth Press.

Hackett, P. (2005) 'Ever Appreciating Circles.' In T.S. Nelson (ed.) *Education and Training in Solution Focused Brief Therapy*. Binghampton, NY: The Howarth Press.

Hawkes, D., Marsh, T.I. and Wilgosh, R. (1998) *Solution Focused Therapy: A Handbook for Health Care Professionals*. Oxford: Butterworth Heinemann.

Henden, J. (2008) *Preventing Suicide: The Solution Focused Approach*. Chichester: Wiley.

Jacob, F. (2001) *Solution Focused Recovery from Eating Distress*. London: BT Press.

Kitwood, T. (1997) *Dementia Reconsidered: The Person Comes First*. Buckingham: Open University Press.

Lamarre, J. (2005) 'Complaining Exercise.' In T.S. Nelson (ed.) *Education and Training in Solution Focused Brief Therapy*. Binghampton, NY: The Howarth Press.

Levy, R. and O'Hanlon, W. (2001) *Try and Make Me: Simple Strategies That Turn Off the Tantrums and Create Co-operation*. Breinigsville, PA: Rodale Books.

Macdonald, A.J. (2011) *Solution-focused Therapy: Theory, Research and Practice* (2nd edn). Sage: London.

McAlistair, M. (2007) 'The Spirit of SFN: Making Change at Three Levels.' In M. McAllister (ed.) *Solution Focused Nursing: Rethinking Practice*. Basingstoke: Palgrave.

Miller, S.D. and Berg, I.K. (1995) *The Miracle Method: A Radically New Approach to Problem Drinking*. New York: W.W. Norton & Co.

Milner, J. (2001) *Women and Social Work: Narrative Approaches*. Basingstoke: Palgrave.

Milner, J. and Bateman, J. (2011) *Working with Children and Teenagers Using Solution Focused Approaches: Enabling Children to Overcome Challenges and Achieve Their Potential*. London: Jessica Kingsley Publishers.

Milner, J. and Jessop, D. (2003) 'Domestic violence: narratives and solutions.' *Probation Journal 50*, 127–141.

Milner, J. and O'Byrne, P. (2002) *Assessment in Social Work* (2nd edn). Basingstoke: Palgrave Macmillan.

Milner, J., Myers, S. and O'Byrne, P. (2015) *Assessment in Social Work 4th Edition*. Basingstoke: Palgrave Macmillan.

Myers, S. (2007) *Solution-focused Approaches*. Lyme Regis: Russell House Press.

Nelson, T. (ed.) (2005) *Education and Training in Solution Focused Brief Therapy*. Binghampton, NY: The Howarth Press.

O'Connell, B. (1998) *Solution Focused Therapy*. London: Sage.

O'Connell, B. (2001) *Solution Focused Stress Counselling*. London and New York: Continuum.

Rycroft, C., Gorer, G., Storr, A., Wren-Lewis, J. and Lomas, P. (1966) *Psychoanalysis Observed*. London: Penguin.

Saleebey, D. (ed) *The Strengths Perspective in Social Work 6th edition.* London: Pearson.

Shennan, G. (2014) *Solution Focused Practice: Effective Communication to Facilitate Change.* Basingstoke: Palgrave.

Swaffer, K. (2015) *What the Hell Happened to my Brain? Living beyond Dementia.* London: Jessica Kingsley Publishers.

Turnell, A. and Essex, S. (2006) *Working with 'Denied' Child Abuse: The Resolutions Approach.* Maidenhead: Open University Press.

Turnell, A. and Lipchik, E. (1999) 'The role of empathy in brief therapy: the overlooked but vital context.' *Australian and New Zealand Journal of Family Therapy 20,* 4177–182.

Walsh, T. (2010) *The Solution Focused Helper: Ethics and Practice in Health and Social Care.* Maidenhead: Open University Press.

White, M. and Epston, D. (1990) *Narrative Means to Therapeutic Ends.* New York: W.W. Norton & Co.

Wright, J. (2003) 'Considering issues of domestic violence and abuse in palliative care and bereavement situations.' *Journal of Narrative Therapy and Community Work 3,* 72–74.

Young, S. (2005) 'Success and Failure.' In T.S. Nelson (ed.) *Education and Training in Solution Focused Brief Therapy.* Binghampton, NY: The Howarth Press.

Index

6, 5, 4, 3, 2, 1 157

A Scaling Walk 120
'Anti Tut Tut Club' 22
Ask the Audience 66
Assessing Confidence 127
assumptions
    about change 25
    about the past 24–5
    about problems 24
    about solutions 25–6
    about talking 25

Back to the Future 107–8, 109
Baker, C. 86–7, 112, 113
Bateman, J. 67, 141
Berg, I.K. 13, 75, 97, 108
Big Brother Diary Room 65
Bridge 110
Brief Therapy Family Center 13

Calendars 119
Can-Do Dinosaurs 105
Cartooning 108
Challenging Problem Talk 61–2
change
    assumptions about 25
child protection 51
    safety assessments 55–7

The three houses 53
Transparency with Adults in Child
    Protection Work 54
Transparency with Children in
    Child Protection Work 52
children
    Ask the Audience 66
    Back to the Future 107–8
    Big Brother Diary Room 65
    Calendars 119
    Customer Complaints Desk 65
    defiant 86
    developing goals 107–8
    Football Bench 65–6
    Helping Hands 166
    Ladders 119
    practice examples 66–7
    scaling progress 119
    Secret Signs 166
    Secret Thoughts Box 166
    starting the conversation with
        65–7
    strengths of 86
    talking to 66–7
    and trauma 158, 166
chronic illnesses 141
comfort cues 161–2
Comfort Cues 163
Communicating Clearly 41
Consulting an Older Wiser Self 109
Couzens, A. 65

Curious Questioning 40, 159
Customer Complaints Desk 65

de Shazer, S. 71, 75
defiant children 86
dementia 86–7
Developing Clear Goals 92
Devising a Task 78
Dilemmas 136
disabilities 141
Dolan, Y. 151, 161, 164
doormat therapy 160–1
double-sided report cards 46

Eliciting Skills 85
Eliciting Strengths 1 88
Eliciting Strengths 2 89
emotions
    From Emotion to Behaviour 1 35
    From Emotion to Behaviour 2 36
    Gerunding! 34
    and solution focused practice 34,
        37–8
    validating 37–8
empathy
    From Emotion to Behaviour 1 35
    From Emotion to Behaviour 2 36
    Gerunding! 34
    and solution focused practice 33–4
end of session tasks 131–2
Epston, D. 68
Essex, S. 52
evaluation sessions 129–30
externalising the problem 68
    Individualising the Problem
        69–71
    practice examples 68
exception finding 46, 58, 71–2
    Exception Finding 73
    practice examples 38, 72
    and pretend tasks 74–6
    question prompts for 74
Exception Finding 73

Fiske, H. 32
Focusing on Strengths 80
Football Bench 65–6
From Emotion to Behaviour 1 35
From Emotion to Behaviour 2 36
From the Past to the Future 111
From Pathologies to Descriptions
    30–1

Gardiner, G. 134
Ghul, R. 61
goal setting 90–1, 111–12
    for adults 109, 110, 111
    Back to the Future 107–8, 109
    Bridge 110
    Cartooning 108
    for children 107–8
    Consulting an Older Wiser Self
        109
    Developing Clear Goals 92
    From the Past to the Future 111
    Goal Setting 113
    miracle question 96–7, 101–5,
        109–10
    nightmare question 97–8
    for people with learning
        difficulties 105–6
    practice examples 111–12
    questions to aid 93, 106–7
    The Miracle Question 99
    for terminally ill people 134–5
    unrealistic goals 100–1
    for violent people 94–5
Goal Setting 113
Good Things 15

Hacket, Paul 29
Hawkes, D. 100, 137
Helping Hands 166
Henden, John 138
Hope from Despair 140

Identifying skills 19–20
Individualising the Problem 69–71

Introductions and Best Hopes 17–18
Invisible Crocodiles 158
Iveson, Chris 19

Jacob, F. 38
Jessop, D. 72

Keeping Solution Focused 63
Kitwood, T. 23

Ladders 119
Lamarre, J. 61
learning difficulties
    goal setting for people with
        105–6
Levy, R. 86
Lipchik, E. 39
listening
    Challenging Problem Talk 61–2
    Communicating Clearly 41
    Curious Questioning 40
    Reframing the Problem/Diagnosis
        44–5
    and solution focused practice 38–9
    Word Watching 1 42
    Word Watching 2 43
living well 164–5

MacDonald, A.J. 59, 78, 119
Marsh, T.I. 100
McAlistair, M. 126
Miller, S.D. 13
Milner, J. 11, 14, 62, 67, 72, 76,
        141, 145
miracle question 96–7, 101–5,
        109–10, 146–7
More Scaling 121
Mr. Men characters 105–6
Myers, S. 11

Nelson, T. 31
nightmare question 97–8

O'Bryne, P. 62, 76, 145
O'Connell, B. 27, 147
Off the Wall Questions 21
O'Hanlon, W. 86

past
    assumptions about 24–5
    people who hear voices 143–5
    Personalising Scaled Questions 128
    poor parenting 151–2
    prediction tasks 76–7
    Devising a Task 78
pretend tasks 74–6
problems
    assumptions about 24
Problems to Solutions 27

recording sessions 49–51
Reframing the Problem/Diagnosis
    44–5
Reuss, H.H. 75, 97
Rogers, C. 33, 37
Rycroft, C. 23

safety
    assessments in child protection
        55–7
    practice examples 55, 116–19
    and violence 153–4
Saleeby, D. 14
scaling progress 114–16
    A Scaling Walk 120
    Assessing Confidence 127
    Calendars 119
    for children 119
    Ladders 119
    More Scaling 121
    Personalising Scaled Questions
        128
    practice example 124–6
    questions for 114–15
    Scaling a Project 123
    Yet More Scaling 122
Scaling a Project 123

Searching for Strengths 84
Secret Signs 166
Secret Thoughts Box 166
selfishness 158
Shazer, Steve de 13
Shennan, G. 115
skills recognition 22
Social Stories 105
solution focused practice
    assumptions of 24–6
    description of 13–14
    emotions 34, 37–8
    empathy 33–4
    Ever Appreciating Circles 28–9
    From Pathologies to Descriptions
        30–1
    listening 38–9
    principles of 22–6, 58
    Problems to Solutions 27
    recording sessions 49–51
    skills recognition in 22
    Solution Focused Scavenger Hunt
        32
    transparency 46
solution focused practice techniques
    asking questions 64
    developing goals 90–1
    end of session tasks 131–2
    evaluation 129–30
    exception finding 71–2
    prediction tasks 76–7
    pretend tasks 74–6
    scaling progress 114–30
    starting the conversation 59–60
    strengths 79
Solution Focused Scavenger Hunt 32
solutions
    assumptions about 25–6
Solutions for You 156
Sparkling Moments 16
starting the conversation 59–60
Steiner, T. 108
strengths 79
    of children 86
    Eliciting Skills 85
    eliciting strengths 82–37

Eliciting Strengths 1 88
Eliciting Strengths 2 89
Focusing on Strengths 80
    of people with dementia 86–7
    practice examples 82
    Searching for Strengths 84
    Success and Failure 81
    of vulnerable people 86–7
strengths based practice
    Good Things 15
    Identifying skills 19–20
    Introductions and Best Hopes
        17–18
    Off the Wall Questions 21
    and solution focused practice 14
    Sparkling Moments 16
stress 146–7
Success and Failure 81
Suicide 137–9
    Hope from Despair 140
Swaffer, Kate 68

talking
    assumptions about 25
terminally people
    Dilemmas 136
    goal setting for 134–5
    main issues of 133–4
The three houses 53
The Miracle Question 99
time therapy 154–5
transparency
    practice examples 49–51
    and solution based practice 46
    The three houses 53
    Transparency 1 47
    Transparency 2 48
    Transparency with Adults in Child
        Protection Work 54
    Transparency with Children in
        Child Protection Work 52
Transparency 1 47
Transparency 2 48
Transparency with Adults in Child
    Protection Work 54

Transparency with Children in Child
  Protection Work 52
trauma
  6,5,4,3,2,1 157
  and children 158, 166
  comfort cues 161–2
  Comfort Cues 163
  Curious Questioning 159
  doormat therapy 160–1
  Helping Hands 166
  impact of 148
  Invisible Crocodiles 158
  living well 164–5
  and poor parenting 151–2
  practice examples 160–1
  Secret Signs 166
  Secret Thoughts Box 166
  and selfishness 158
  Solutions for You 156
  survival questions 150
  time therapy 154–5
  and treats 164
treats 164

Try and Make Me! (Levy and
  O'Hanlon) 86
Turnell, A. 39, 52

unrealistic goals 100–1

violence
  control of 153–4
  practice examples 149, 150–1
  and safety 153–4

Walsh, T. 133, 135, 140
White, M. 68
Wilgosh, R. 100
Word Watching 1 42
Word Watching 2 43
Wright, J. 135

Yet More Scaling 122

Zalter, B. 32

Previously a senior lecturer in social work, **Judith Milner** recently retired from work as a therapist, consultant and independent expert to family courts in child protection, domestic violence and contested contact cases. She is widely published on solution focused practice. **Steve Myers** is Director of Social Sciences at University of Salford, Manchester. A social work academic since 1995, he has led research projects and has authored and co-authored a series of books and articles about violence, sex and solutions. Judith and Steve both live in Yorkshire.